Build Your Own Hot Tub With Concrete

BY MARVIN E. JOHNSON

Copyright © 1985 Marvin E. Johnson

All rights reserved.

ISBN: 1499504918

ISBN-13: 978-1499504910

DEDICATION

COLOSSIANS 3, VERSE 17

"And whatsoever ye do in word or deed, do all in the Hand of the Lord Jesus, giving thanks to God and the Father by him."

SPECIAL THANKS TO:

My wife and family for their support.

Seattle-King County Department of Public Health.

Rob Kampbell of Emcon, Incorporated, Tacoma, Washington.

CONTENTS

	Preface	i
1	Why Build Your Own Spa?	1
2	Permits and Taxes	2
3	Preparation	3
4	The Hole	5
5	Anchor Bolts	20
6	Steel Reinforcing	27
7	What Size Spa?	29
8	Build Forms	35
9	Adding a Step	42
10	Plumbing	50
11	Jets	56
12	Bubbler	70
13	Air Buttons	79
14	Electrical	87
15	Outer Dam	95
16	Pouring the Concrete	97
17	Painting and Tiling	104
18	Supporting Equipment	115
19	Equipment Pad	117
20	Pump House	121
21	Room, Skirts, and Decks	126
22	Staying Happy and Healthy In Your Spa	141
23	Using Leftover Concrete	163

PREFACE

This book is a general guide that shows how to create and build your own spa from scratch using concrete, steel and tile; the most durable materials around.

You can save half the cost of hiring a professional and take pride in a project that will serve you for years. Your own basic home tools are all that are needed.

Although all possible measures have been taken to ensure the accuracy of the materials presented, neither the author, Wishing Well Spas, nor the printer is liable in case of misinterpretation of directions, misapplication or typographical errors. Individuals using this book should submit their plans and construction to local building inspectors for final approval.

1 ~ WHY BUILD YOUR OWN SPA?

1. This book is a source of information and shows you how to build a concrete spa from scratch. You will save over half the cost of hiring a professional.

2. Use common tools. Because you pour the concrete, no special equipment is used. Anyone can build their own spa or small pool.

3. In this world of plastic, you may want something that will really last. Concrete is one of the most durable and versatile materials to work with. It is ideal for spas.

4. Value. A properly made concrete and tiled spa will add value to your home and years of carefree enjoyment.

5. To make money. You can build these spas for extra income or add an extra dimension to your pool or spa business.

6. A great project. People build homes, boats, etc. Why not your spa?

7. Is it hard? For some, yes, but for a person that has a little knowledge of building, it's just another project. Pay attention and follow the instructions. Use common sense.

8. Is this a weekend project? No. If you work a regular job, expect at least 2 months of your spare time.

9. For health and recreation.

10. A concrete spa can be built in an existing room without removing walls while avoiding other problems that may present themselves with installation of large pre-formed shells.

2 ~ PERMITS AND TAXES

It is your responsibility to submit your plans and obtain a building permit, meet local codes, and provide security.

Have a qualified electrician do your electrical work and insist on inspections. ALL metal in, on, or around a pool should be grounded. An electrical inspector will show you if you are in doubt. All spa lights must be on a G.F.I.

Property taxes are a factor you may have to contend with.

Check with your tax accountant or the IRS if you have a medical problem. You can, in some situations, deduct your spa and operating expenses.

3 ~ PREPARATION

Some things to consider:

1. Soil type and water drainage. If you have an unusual soil condition, underground springs, swamp, sand or wet clay, seek the advice of a local builder.

2. Underground obstructions. Tree roots, septic tanks, pipes, etc. It is recommended that your local utility company identify and mark any underground electrical.

3. Security. Safeguarding for small children and pets.

4. Protecting from weather, dirt and vegetation. A good cover will solve most of these problems.

5. Access for concrete truck. Use a small pumper or plan on using a wheelbarrow.

6. Access to electrical and/or gas for support equipment. Your electrician and/or utility company can help you. Where you locate your equipment is important. See the chapter on equipment.

7. Draining your spa. A gravity drain is best in most cases. A small pump is also an excellent way to drain. The pump on your spa equipment may be used. The wastewater from a spa is a relatively small amount. You can drain it into your garden or lawn unless there are local restrictions.

8. Ventilation. Your spa, when in use, will create a lot of moisture. If you enclose it in a room, you will have to provide ventilation with at least a 10" fan or opening windows or both. Chlorine may build up in the air, causing breathing problems - another reason for adequate ventilation. Most enclosed spas have their own small room for this reason. In addition, this type of ventilation won't vacate heat from your house. Some use dehumidifiers to remove moisture from the spa room, which work fine, and you don't loose the heat in your home or the building.

9. Future plans. Many enclose their spas. However, this can be done at a later date. The first year you may build your spa in a deck or a separate patio. The following year put a roof or gazebo over it. Maybe an awning. If you roof over your spa then at a later date you can add walls with windows; then at a later date you can finish the room off with cedar and tile, etc. By doing your spa and room in stages you may elect to stop with only a roof over it, and you may decide you don't need or want walls. You won't have to outlay too much money at one time. If you are going to borrow from a bank, you may be better off doing the whole project at one time. Give it some thought. Talk it over with friends that own a spa.

Note: A heated room is not necessary. In fact, a cool or even cold room is preferred while using a hot tub. When a spa is not in use, and properly covered, there is no longer any moisture loss.

4 ~ THE HOLE

Once you decide where your spa is going to be located, you will prepare the hole. If you are going to put your spa in a deck, you cut a hole that will allow at least 6" thick concrete walls. If your forms measure 6' across (the form patterns shown in this book will measure 6'), then your hole will measure 7' across, plus an area for steps.

This chapter contains pictures and information. The basic construction steps are explained in later chapters.

You will probably build your forms prior to digging the hole. I'm writing this the same way I install a spa. First I prepare the site, set anchor bolts, add rebar and ground wire, set seats, tile, drill air holes, install equipment, build pump house and covers, make final electrical and gas connections; then fill with water and it's done.

This hole is through an existing patio. Plumbing will all come through the hole in the center of this photo. The drain line and light conduit are in. Other plumbing will be added when the forms are set in place.

Building on the ground: You will need to pour a small collar (patio) or jackhammer through an existing one. The collar is poured before the hole is dug. The dirt hole actually becomes your outer form. If the dirt is really loose, you will need some forming to keep it from caving in.

This picture shows the patio, the hole, the forms (in the background), a false bottom with "J" bolts, and 6 bags of pre-mix concrete to anchor bolts. The 2' x 4's overhead are used to build a plastic enclosure for rainy weather protection after the cement is poured.

This hole was partially formed up because of stumps that had to be removed. The collar (patio) is about 4' wide and approximately 15' across. Plywood is used so dirt could be back-filled. Before the patio was poured, a trench was dug for plumbing. The patio drops approximately 1 1/2" for water run-off.

Next, you need to know how far or how high you want the top edge of the spa to be.

The top edge of this spa is 6" above the floor. Many are 3 1/2" high.

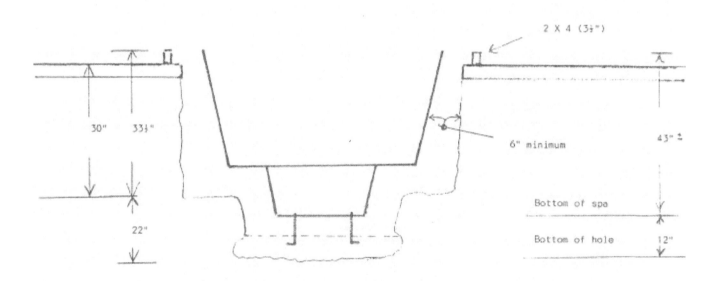

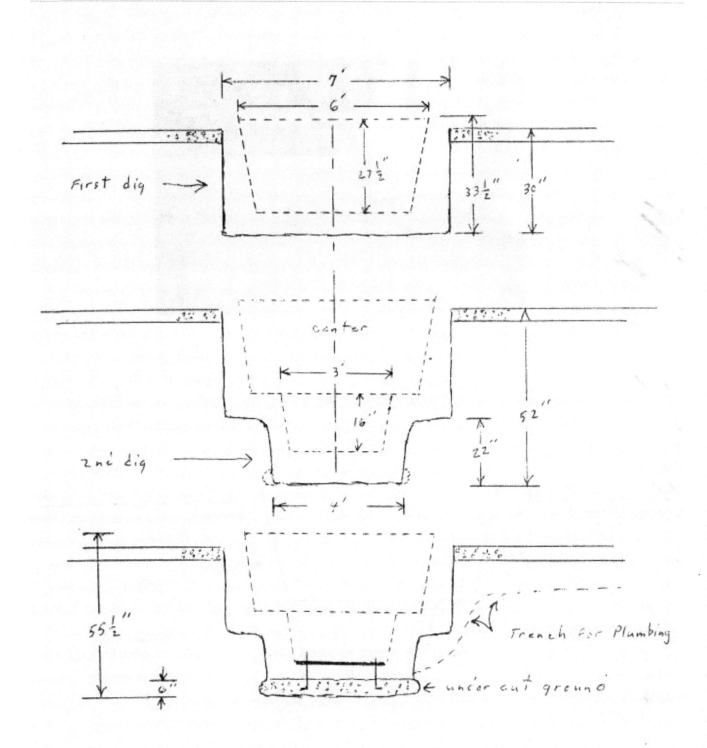

If you want to build your spa in deck and the hole dimensions are the same as the previous in-ground examples, the only difference will be that part of the hole is formed up with plywood instead of dirt.

When considering how deep to dig the hole, your forms will measure approximately 43" from top to bottom.

The form for the foot well is 16". The form for the seating when finished is 27" so the inside dimensions are 43"*. (See the chapter on forms.) You will probably build the forms before making the actual hole that the spa will be in.

*2 x 4 collar added.

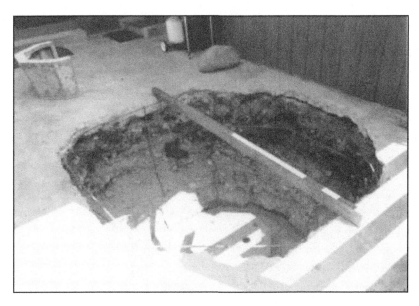

The anchor bolts and rebar are in place.

The top of this tub will be 3 1/2" above the patio deck. From the top of the 2 x 4 to the bottom of spa is 43".

The tunnel and trench for a gravity drain.

Note: If a gravity drain is going to be installed, or the equipment will be alongside your spa, then you will need to tunnel and trench as part of digging the hole.

The tunnel and trench for plumbing to support equipment. The wood is removed prior to pouring spa.

If you are going to add steps, you must plan them before pouring the patio. After the plumbing is installed and thoroughly tested, concrete will cover this walk area.

The main hole is dug (or formed), then plumbing is started and the anchor bolts are added. It should be noted here that the anchor bolts are what make it possible to pour a concrete spa in one continuous pour (monolithic). A monolithic pour eliminates seams that would leak. The anchor bolts also simplify holding the forms in place during the pour.

If building in an upper deck, you will have to form a pedestal to support your spa. Half of this deck was dropped to allow headroom.

The footings are poured first. The center will be filled with dirt then the walls and top will be poured.

This sketch represents the pedestal for an upper deck spa.

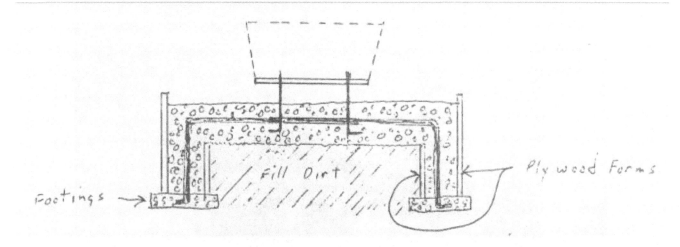

The drainpipe in this example follows the trench dug on the right side of the photo.

The anchor bolts will hold the inside forms. The octagon board represents the bottom of the foot well.

This spa was poured the hard way. The concrete was wheeled to the deck then lifted in 5 gallon buckets - which took 2 people about 3 hours.

The boxes in the photo are block-outs to reduce the amount of concrete needed.

5 ~ ANCHOR BOLTS

This is one of the most important steps. It really is the secret to success. When I first made my own concrete spa, I was confronted with the problem of holding my forms in place. I knew the tremendous force wet concrete exerts on the forms. The forms were going to try to float up. I figured it was necessary to hold the bottom of the forms, but how? Believe me, I worked on this a long time. I finally came up with an idea. A bolt system which will be explained further. The "J" bolts will serve two purposes: First, to anchor the forms; second, to allow the concrete to flow under and around the forms and encase all the plumbing.

These bolts are in place and ready to receive the forms. They extend 9" above the concrete. This concrete should cure for at least one week.

This is another method that is only used to explain the basic concept. 12 inch "J" bolts are what I use now, with rebar wired on. Rebar is welded or wired to the bottom of the bolts. The concrete holding the bolts is usually green. The rebar is added insurance that they won't pull apart.

The anchor bolts are in place.

The foot well is in place on top of the anchor bolts. The drain is positioned away from where the step will be located.

The bolts used are 12 inch "J" bolts. These are available at most lumber and material stores. To position the bolts you can make a board that represents the bottom of the foot well. When cutting your foot well forms, you just cut two bottoms. Drill 4 holes (1/2") in each board, preferably on the edge of your forms so that they penetrate the 2 x 4's. See illustration.

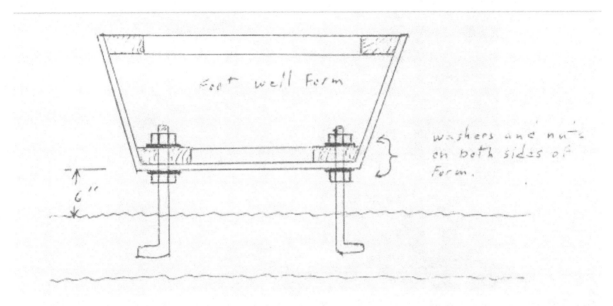

The holes on the false bottom match the bolt holes on the foot well forms.

The bolts should go through the plywood form and the 2 x 4's inside the forms, otherwise, the bolts could tear loose under the strain of pouring the concrete.

This picture shows the false bottom used to position the anchor bolts and the drain. A depression was made for the main drain, pipes, and fittings so that all will be encapsulated with at least 6" of concrete. This will seal the pipes and fittings and prevent leakage. The board must be centered and level, and over 6" above the concrete.

Placing the Bolts

Now that the false bottom with "J" bolts is in place, you need to locate them. The board must be centered, level, and properly aligned. Since it represents the bottom surface of your spa, it has to be the right depth.

The bolts and drain are in place. The hole is filled with 6" of concrete, then the board with bolts and drain are positioned. The drain can be added later if you wish; just make sure you have sufficient clearance for the type of drain used. In this photo, the drain is in place and plumbed. The pipe shown is for the skimmer.

Note: The opening of all pipes and fittings are covered with duct tape to prevent any dirt from entering the plumbing.

The depth for the spa bottom will be the height of your forms (43") minus the height you plan above ground. Measure your forms and allow for the thickness of the plywood.

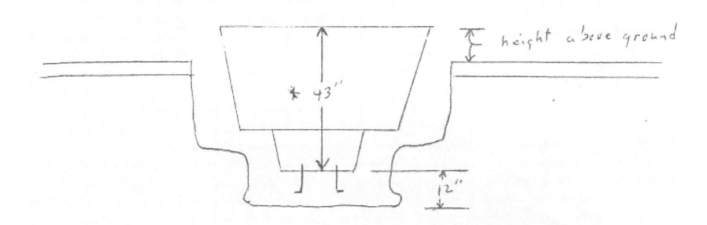

The boards were removed and trench was filled with dirt before the final pour was made.

6 ~ STEEL REINFORCING

Rebar (steel reinforcing) gives your concrete extra strength. I use 3/8" thick rebar because I can bend it by hand. Keep the rebar close to the outside of your hole for better strength and to allow clearance for your forms and plumbing - which will stick out 4" from the forms. The rebar pattern here is about 12" squares. If local code requires, you may have to wire your rebar and/or size it to restrictions.

The rebar is going into place. This is a good time to bond the rebar which must have a ground wire attached. See the chapter on electrical.

Steps can be added to your forms. This box for the step is 10" deep by 18" wide and 10" above the seat. The first step is only a few inches below floor level. See the chapter on steps. Keep this in mind when designing your spa and plumbing the hole.

7 ~ WHAT SIZE SPA?

Before we get into the actual construction, let's ponder a few points. If you use my form pattern, you will have a basic, standard size spa. What is standard? That point can be argued indefinitely, but let's be practical and average the tubs on the market. These sizes have been developed by trial and error and by what appeals to the general public. The beauty of a custom built tub is the fact that you can design a tub to suit your own ideas. The forms in this book reflect a few features I prefer that most plastic spas don't offer. I like a foot well that is between 16" and 18" deep. This makes your spa much roomier. A 16" foot well depth is adequate for the average person, while a 20" depth is preferable for the very tall. I have built one with a 25" foot well.

This is the first spa that I cast. It was, and is, my test bed. That's my son, Bill, and my daughter, RaeAnn, testing it out - very serious work.

This spa is extremely basic and does not have built-in steps, which are nice but not necessary.

I prefer the height of the seat back to be between 26" and 28".

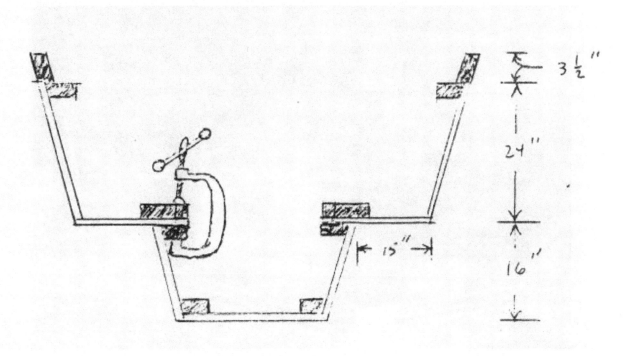

I like a water depth at seating level between 19" to 22", so when I'm sitting in the spa the water just covers my shoulders. I'm 5'8".

The seat should be approximately 15" wide. If you want to customize the dimensions, sit in a chair and measure how deep you would like it. The top edge of the spa should not be higher than the base of your neck. The water level should be approximately 7" below the top of the spa. The total water depth will be approximately 36".

WARNING: Small children can be in serious trouble in water that deep

My sister, MaryAnn, is 5'3" and my brother-in-law Bob is 6'3". My daughter, RaeAnn wears water-wings, and my niece, Kristine, has foggy glasses.

This size spa is adequate for the average family.

If you want to control the water level, you can plumb in an overflow. Also, a couple of seats can be elevated. Remember, the more people that get in the spa, the higher the water level rises until it overflows. This size spa will hold 6 average size adults. The water naturally rises, but not so deep that it would cover an adult's face, and when they get out you haven't lost all your water. There will be that occasional party when too many will be in your tub and you will have to replace some water when they exit the spa. Again, this size spa is fine for the average family while large enough to invite some friends. Your spa is not so big that your operating costs and equipment get out of hand. Some families want a larger spa and the same principals apply in construction, however the equipment to operate it has to be larger and the plumbing changes. This gets more involved as the size of the spa increases.

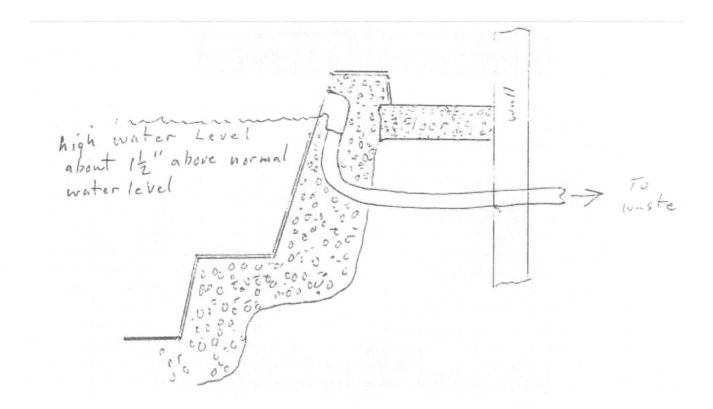

An overflow is nothing more than a 1 1/2" to 2" pipe that allows water to spill out if too many people enter. Set the bottom of the pipe at the level you want water to start overflowing. I usually have a removable cap that offers the option of not allowing any water to escape.

This swim spa was constructed with the same principals as my smaller units. A future publication on larger spas, including swim spas which measure 8' x 14' or 16', will follow this book.

The swim spa equipment room: Equipment on larger spas changes dramatically, as does the cost.

8 ~ BUILD THE FORMS

Patterns and Materials:

Patterns in this chapter are for a standard size hot tub. Build your own forms with a minimum of 5/8" plywood. You will need three 4 x 8 sheets. If you plan more than one tub, you may want to invest in form guard plywood and make forms that break down. The forms described in this chapter are torn apart after the pour is made, and are not planned for reuse.

Brace your forms with 2 x 4's (approximately 50 feet will be needed) and 2 x 8's (approximately 16 feet). Study the photos. Scrap plywood is used to strengthen the corners. This will give you strong forms that are still light enough for a couple of people to lift.

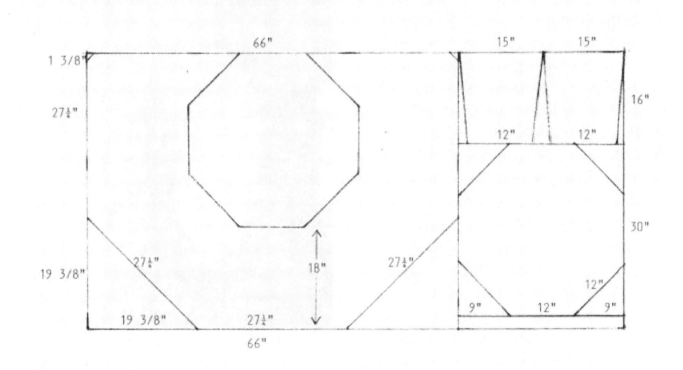

BUILD YOUR OWN HOT TUB WITH CONCRETE

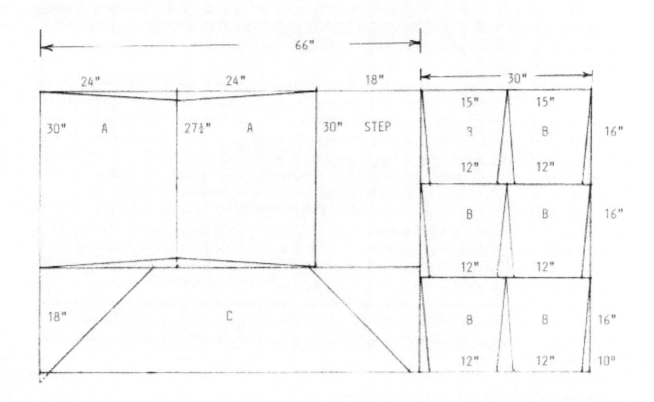

All edges are reinforced with 2 x 4's and 2 x 8's. If you have built forms before, you are aware of the force concrete can exert.

These forms are designed to be torn apart and scrapped. All holes are filled prior to use.

The blocked out area on the back wall is for a box-type skimmer.

Notice the bracing. The 2 x 4's across the outside are temporary and are used to position the forms in the hole and to position the anchor bolts. This method can be used instead of building a special board to position the bolts as shown in the chapter on anchor bolts. The four holes in the bottom of the foot well are inspection holes. Inspection holes are only necessary for very stiff concrete.

The concrete walls are extra thick (12"). The step is built in. Beveled molding was added, narrowing the top to 10".

Notice the 2 x 4's on top of the form. The outer dam is made from 2 x 8's and canted in to add a more desirable shape. Molding can be added to round the beveled edges.

Clamping a guide board will give you accurate cuts. The saw is set at 22 1/2° for an octagon. You will use this angle on most of your work.

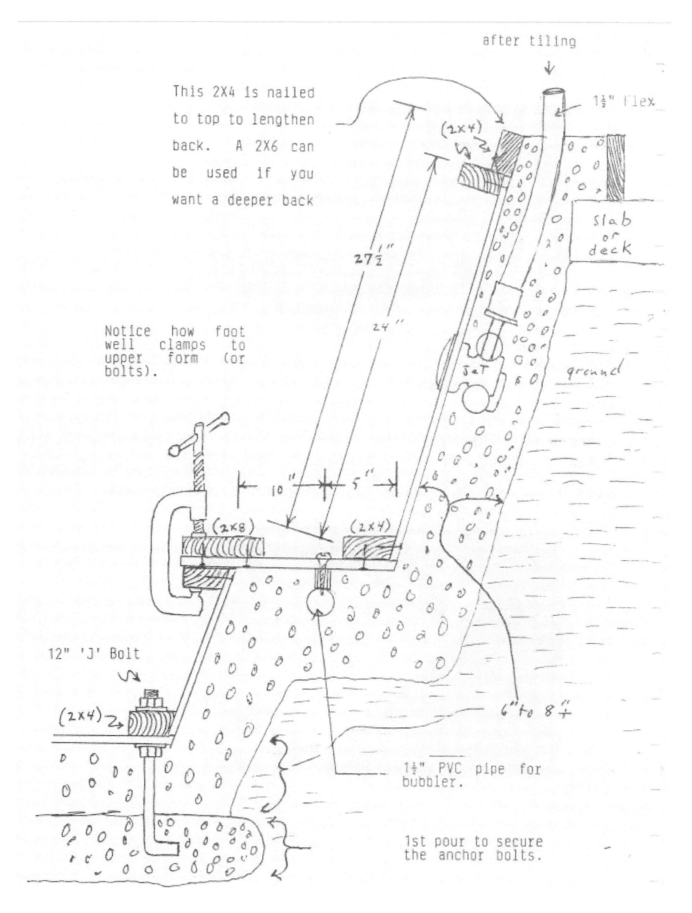

9 ~ ADDING A STEP

Some spas have steps and some do not. The rules that apply to swimming pools generally apply to spas. If you are building a spa for commercial use, then you must study the regulations pertaining to your area. This book is not intended to be the sole source of information for commercial application or local restrictions. The general rule is to provide adequate entry and exit from your pool whether it's a ladder or steps. The rules are flexible in most areas. A normal step in a home will have a 9" rise and a 10" or 12" tread.

This size step is a little large for most home spas, so you may want to modify them for your own personal use. To avoid any legal hassle, the following pictures will give you an idea of different methods for adding steps. The measurements are up to you.

Remember, this chapter is only on how to add a step.

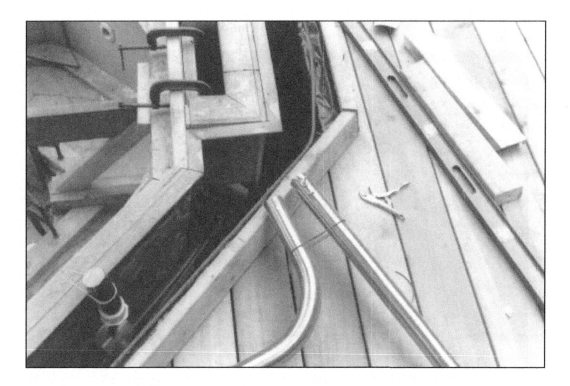

The step is a box clamped or nailed to the side of your forms. The outside shape of the hole and outer dam will change depending on what type of step you want.

Different spas, similar step applications.

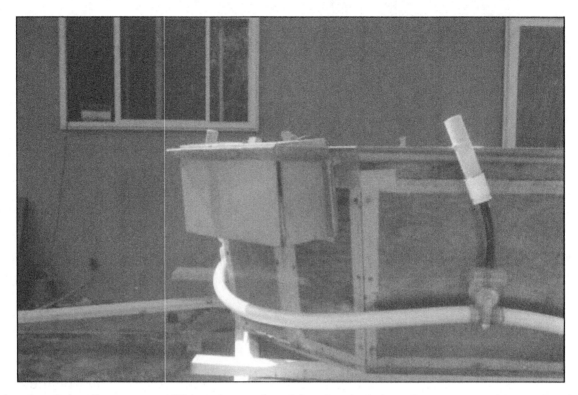

The depth of the first step will be determined by the height of your spa above the deck or floor. Most people can negotiate stepping down 10". When adding inside steps, you can split the difference. A step should be at least 20" wide and 10" tread width.

Some prefer only one step. Extra steps and a grab rail add extra safety and are highly recommended.

IMPORTANT!

When adding internal steps or when bonding fresh concrete to old or cured concrete, you must use a bonding agent. One method is to make a paste from thin set mortar mixed with acrylic and painting the surface of cured concrete. Before the paste dries, pour your steps. This method is also used when adding mortar to elevate seats or topping mix to level the top surface of the spa prior to tiling. This is necessary every time mortar is bonded to cured concrete in order to prevent a "cold joint."

These steps take up room. Not everyone wants them. However, they are nice for older people or the not so nimble. They may be very important.

Adding steps and grab rails make entry and exit very safe and easy. Pea gravel mix is used for the steps and topping mix is used to elevate the seats.

The top step appears long. The step is measured from the floor and not the top of the spa.

IMPORTANT! If you plan to add a step in the foot well, locate your drain away from the step. Remember to allow for the light fixture.

This step is 9" high and divides the seat width. The top step is approximately 20" wide.

Some eliminate the step in the foot well to allow more room for feet. However, if elevated seating is added the step is not a hindrance and it gives the kids a footrest.

Welcome!

10 ~ PLUMBING

The basics:

There are 4 major items plumbed to the spa:

1. Pipe from drain and skimmer to suction end of pump.

2. Pipe return, from equipment to spa jets.

3. Pipe from blower to bubbler ring under seat.

4. Air vent to jets.

There are 4 minor items plumbed to the spa:

1. Air switch tubes.

2. Spa light 3/4" tubing to power source.

3. Overflow line.

4. Automatic filler line.

The minor items are optional and can be eliminated. The air switches are often mounted on a deck or a wall whenever possible. They are subject to wear and must occasionally be replaced.

> **IMPORTANT!**
> The drain of your spa must be an approved type and coupled with another drain or a skimmer to prevent possible serious injury.

Basics for a Spa

Let's start with the drain and skimmer. The drain serves two functions:

It is the beginning of water circulation. Water is drawn from the main bottom drain and the skimmer to the suction end of the pump. The water is forced out of the pump through the filter, through the heater, and back to the spa via the jets. If the situation allows it, a gravity drain can be added to this line. An approved drain designed for a spa should be used. These are anti-cyclonic to prevent hair entanglement, which could be a serious problem.

The drain must be coupled with a skimmer or another outlet which prevents anyone from becoming stuck to an operating drain, something that could also be very serious. By drawing water from two outlets, should the cover be removed by accident and you come into contact with an unguarded outlet, you would be able to pull free without injury.

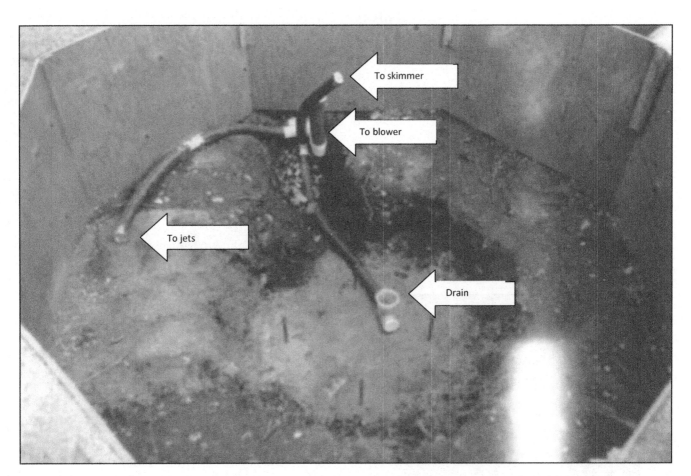

These photos show the main drain, coupled with a pipe for the skimmer.

The pipe on the left alongside the plywood is the jet line. The pipe on the right is the 2" line for the bubbler. Flexible pipe is used because it is much easier to maneuver than rigid pipe.

This type of skimmer is centered 5" below the water line.

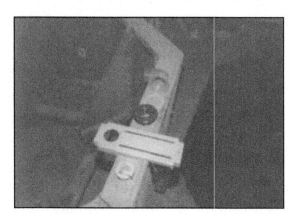

This type of skimmer replaces the box type for spas.

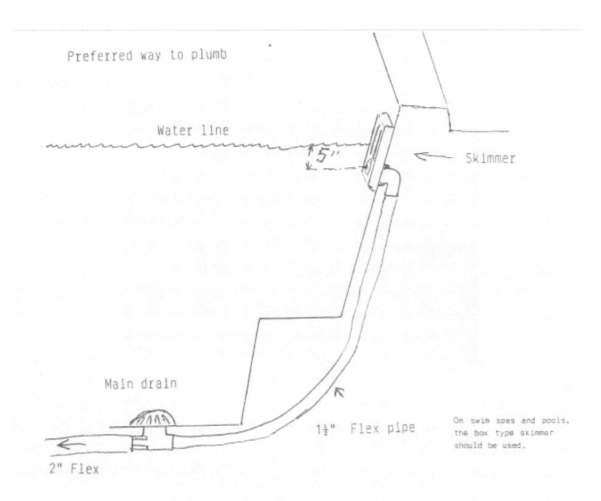

On swim spas and pools, the box type skimmer should be used. The photo below shows the plumbing that attaches the drain to the skimmer.

The complete suction system is shown here. The bottom two are suction fittings. The top fitting is to the skimmer. The light niche is also shown. This spa is drained through the plumbing. It will drain all but 3" on the bottom. Plastic spas almost always have side drains, and a concrete spa can be plumbed the same way. However, by using a bottom drain you will be able to empty all the water when draining.

This is NOT the way to plumb your drain. You will get too much suction on the skimmer. This may pull air into the pump every time the water is just slightly low or whenever you turn the pump on high speed. When trying to empty the spa with the pump, you will definitely start sucking air via the skimmer before the spa is empty.

Note: "Action" on a spa skimmer is not as important as a swimming pool.

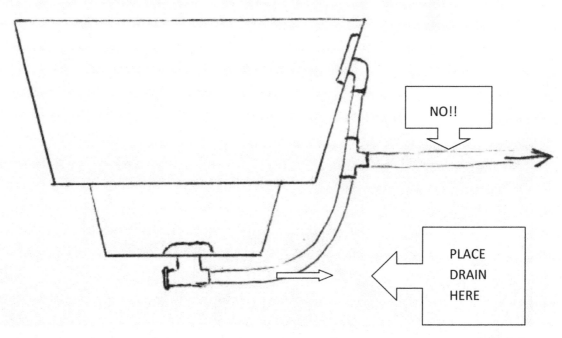

I don't recommend plumbing in this manner because the only way to completely drain your tub is with a wet-vacuum or some other form of suction.

Label all of your plumbing with a permanent marker and arrows showing the direction of water flow from start to finish. As in:

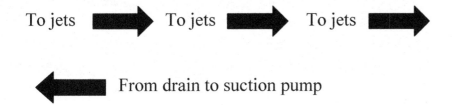

11 ~ THE JETS

The jets make a hot tub a spa.

The jets not only provide the therapy action, but they also return the water taken from the drain to the spa. This completes the circulation cycle. In some spas, or swim spas, this may not be the case but in a typical spa they are both water return and therapy jets. A rule of thumb: You should have 1/4 h.p. per jet. In other words, if you have a one horse pump your spa should have no more than 4 jets. I prefer a 1 1/2 h.p. pump and 4 or 5 jets on the standard size spa, or 2 h.p. for 7 jets. This gives you good strong jets and enough jets for most situations. When you are using a spa it is just as important to get away from the jets as it is to have one massage you. People will move around. The point is, you don't have to over-jet the spa. In fact, 4 jets are plenty for a standard octagon.

A typical jet:

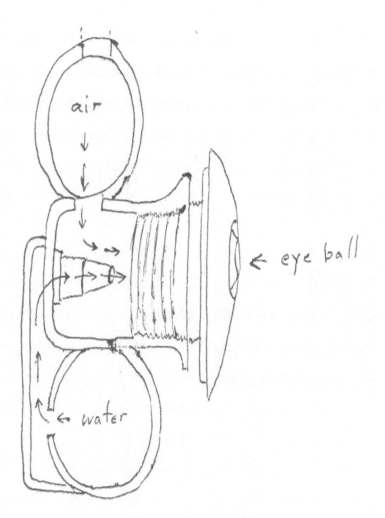

Air can enter via individual air vents or they can be coupled together with one vent supplying several jets.

How they work: The jet is a venturi jet. When the water is forced through the jet nozzle, a vacuum is formed around the jet. When air vents are opened, air is sucked into the jet stream. You do not hook the blower up to the jets.

These jets, with individual air vent pipes, are ready for the concrete pour. The top pipe is taped to keep dirt out. After the tub is tiled, it will be cut off and the air vent cap will be installed.

When water is forced through a jet, and the air vents are closed, you won't feel much thrust from the jets. The reason for this is because the stream of water is penetrating a solid body of water. When you open an air vent, the air being introduced foams the water and the stream of water from the jet can penetrate foamed water easier than solid water, therefore the thrust feels much stronger.

By controlling the amount of air, you control the thrust of your jets; this way they are adjustable. Many spas have the air chambers of jets plumbed together to only one air vent opening. This works fine, and in some applications, should be done this way. However, whenever the situation allows, I prefer individual air controls on each jet. There are jets which you can control from the eyeball. The idea is okay, but most that I have seen have one or two drawbacks, so I still use the air vents on top of the spas. In the future I may change if I find the right one.

Plumbing jet for individual air vent. Water pipe is on the bottom. Note: Most plumbing kits available have detailed instructions.

Placement of Jets

In a home spa, you should put jets at various heights. Let's say your water depth is 22" from the seat to the surface. One jet should be 18" (approximately) above the seat or 4" below the water surface. This jet is for the neck and shoulders and will be the most sought after jet, so you may want two at this position. If you center a jet too close to the surface, it may shoot water out of the spa. Next, a couple of mid-range jets from 8" to 13"; if you want a standard height, stay 11" to 12" above the seat. Also, put one jet 4" above the seat. This jet will hit the lower back and if you sit with your legs straight across you can put your feet against this jet; pure heaven for aching feet! I prefer a jet in this manner instead of placing one in the foot well, because you only massage your feet a couple of minutes and a jet in the foot well is hard to get away from. Also, they usually are inefficient because of the greater back pressure.

The water pipe is on the bottom. This is the return line from your equipment to the jets. Water enters at a 'T' in the line.

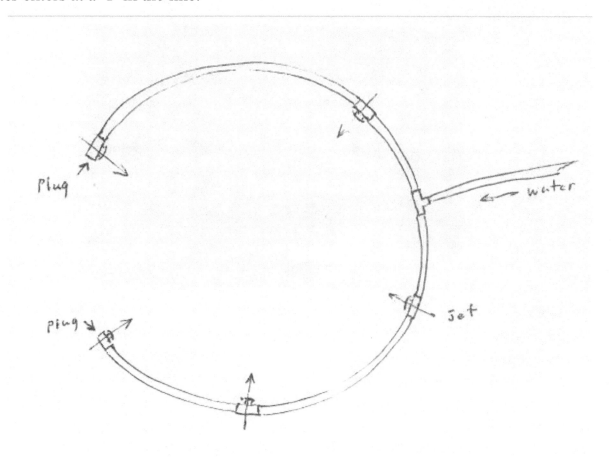

Keep in mind when you build your own spa that you can place jets to massage a particular spot you want. If you want to you can double up on a jet.

Before I plumb a tub I have people sit in a chair, and by pressing their back you can measure the height exactly. If they are undecided, I will place one 4" below the surface, three of them mid-range and one 4" above the seat. If you are planning to elevate any seat, this will change the spot the jet hits you. You can put all jets 12" above the seat.

These instructions will cover most basic installations.

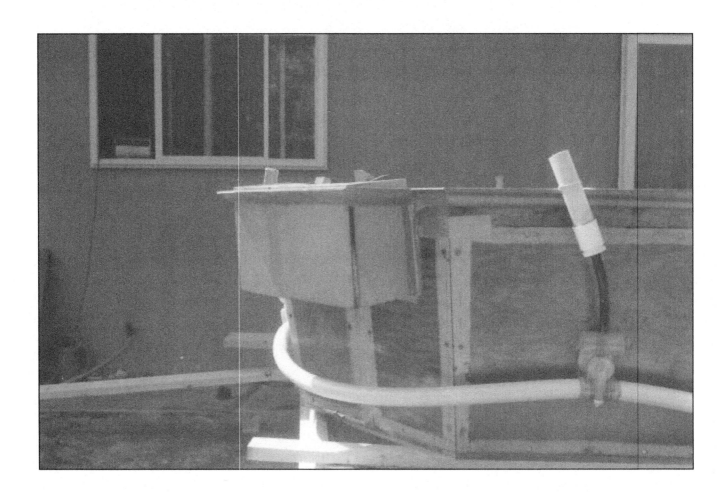

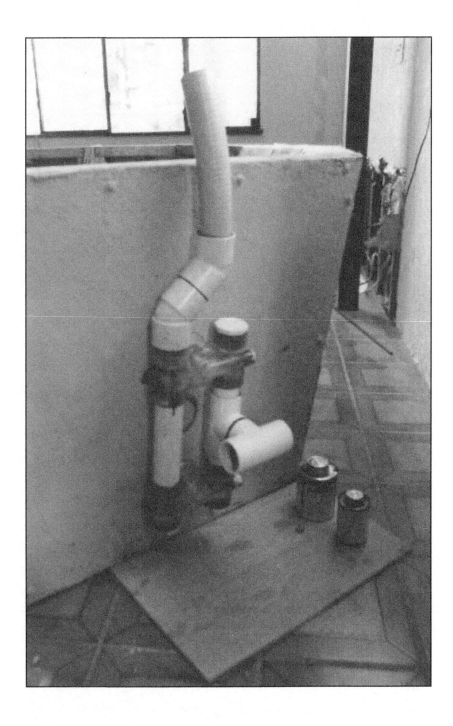

Two jets can be plumbed together. The water side has the "T". Notice where the plugs go. The air vents are plumbed differently. Two "45's" are used to center the air line directly over jets in order to match the appearance of the other jets.

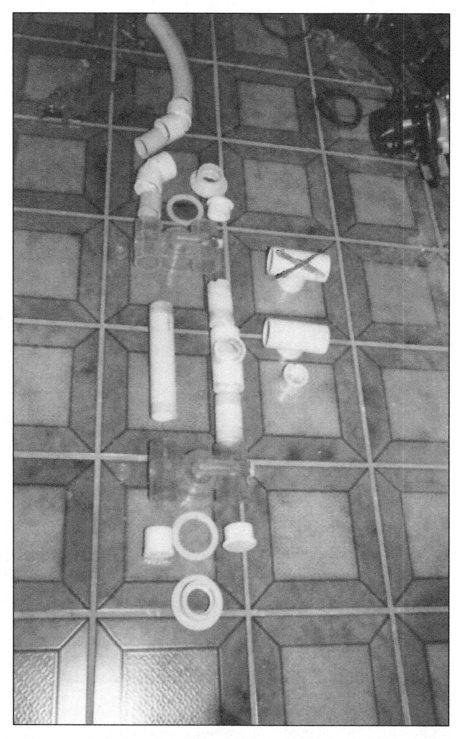

Take your time if you plumb two jets together. All openings must be plugged. This photo has an extra 'T' shown that isn't needed. Remember, if you start adding more jets, you may want a larger water pump (at least 1/4 h.p. per jet). Pumps of 2 h.p. are just about the maximum you can use with 1 1/2" and 2" pipe.

If multi-jets are used, then you must divide the load from the pump or pumps. Extra suction should be added so you don't starve one large or multiple pumps.

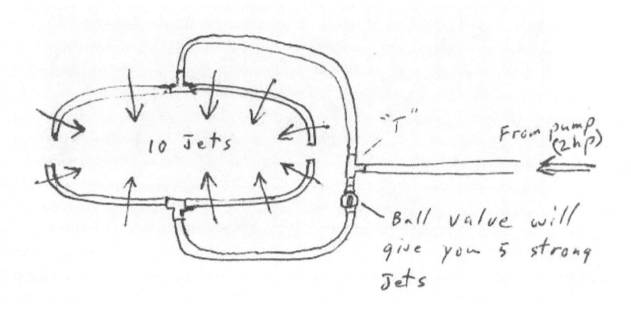

Arrows indicate jets.

Circled are: A 'T' is in place so one pump can run several jets. This way you can try it with one large pump. This 'T' is located so you can get at it. If you add another pump, you simply remove the 'T' and plumb a pump to each side, or add a valve that will divert the flow to one side only. The disadvantage with the valve is that one side is shut down.

Remember, if you use large pumps (2 h.p. or larger), or you think you might add on other pumps, then plumb in additional suction fitting. Make sure additional suctions are in pairs or plumbed in a way to prevent anyone from being stuck to a single outlet.

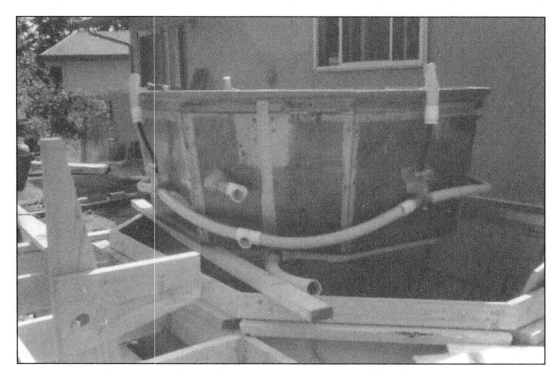

This photo shows jets plumbed and the 'T' where the inlet goes. Air vents in place in this tub are made of 1/2" flex pipe so the vents can be centered prior to the concrete curing. The skimmer will plumb to the main drain and return to equipment. The pipe next to the 2 x 4 is to the blower and bubbler line under the seats.

Notice the plug on the end jet.

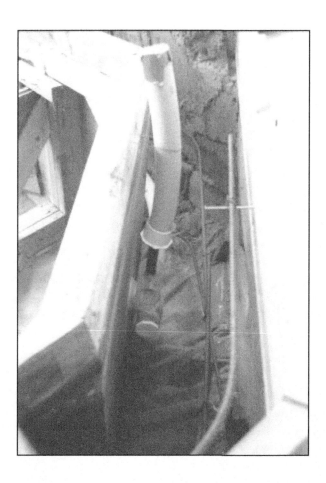 

After pouring concrete, the air vents are centered. Notice tape to keep the pipes clear of concrete. It is important, prior to pouring the concrete, that all openings are taped off to keep debris out.

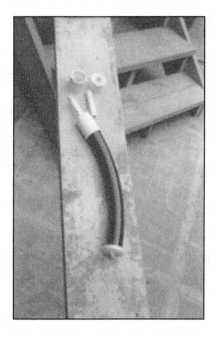

12 ~ BUBBLER

The bubbler adds extra enjoyment. It can also cool the tub down if it gets too hot.

~ ~ ~

The bubbler is an important part of a spa. You can get by without one, but it's like owning a car without a radio. Many of the portables eliminate the blower because the smaller heaters can't keep up with the heat loss while the blower is in use.

Very simply; the bubbler is a pipe with holes drilled in it and a blower attached.

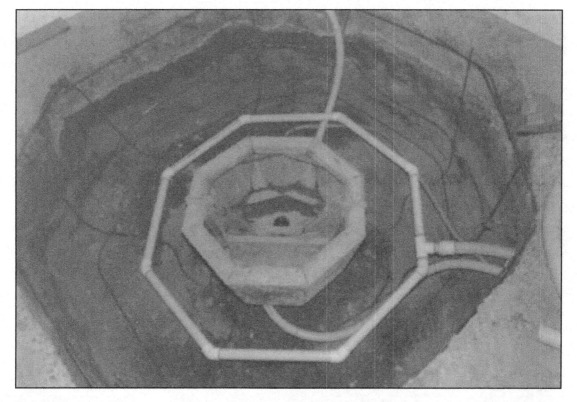

The bubbler is made from 1 1/2" PVC SCH 40 pipe. The line from the blower to the 'T' in the bubbler is 2" flex. There is also a check valve in this line to prevent water from flooding the 2" line, which would make the blower work too hard.

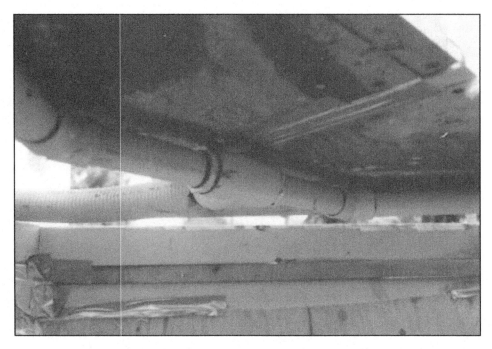

The bubbler line is attached under the seat form.

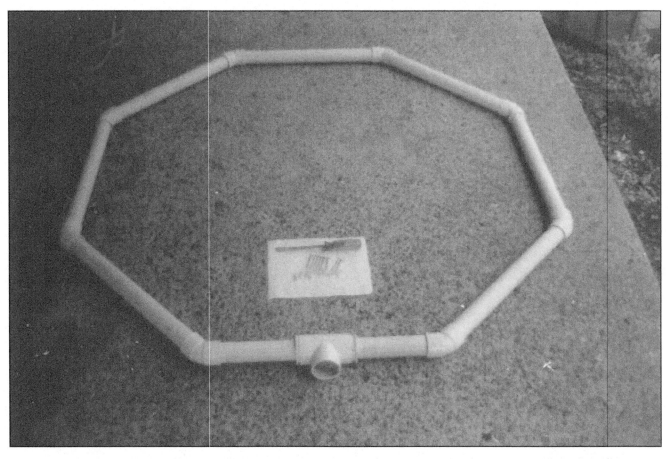

Screws and tubes for spacers (1 1/2") are used to attach the ring to the forms.

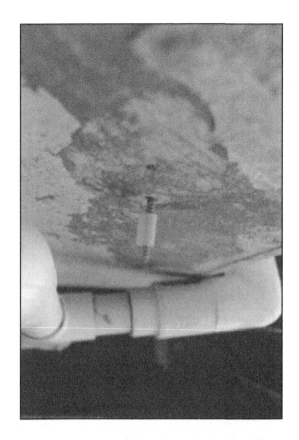 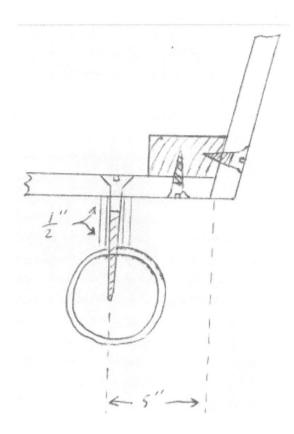

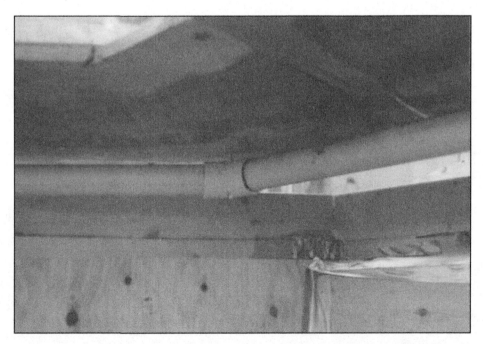

The pipe is 1/2" below the form bottom and 5" from the outer edge of form. Actually, you can locate a bubbler from the front edge of the seat to within 5" of the seat back.

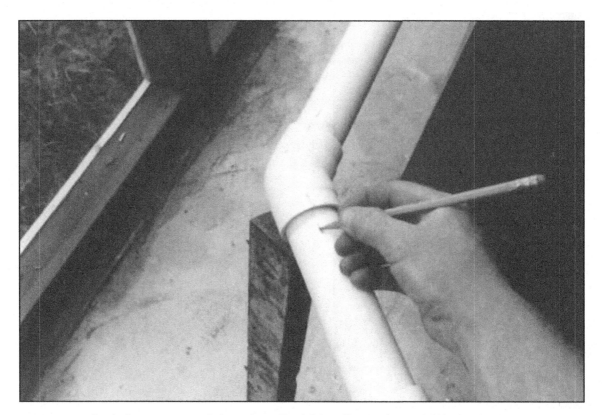

Find the center of the pipe (bubbler line) then drill the holes.

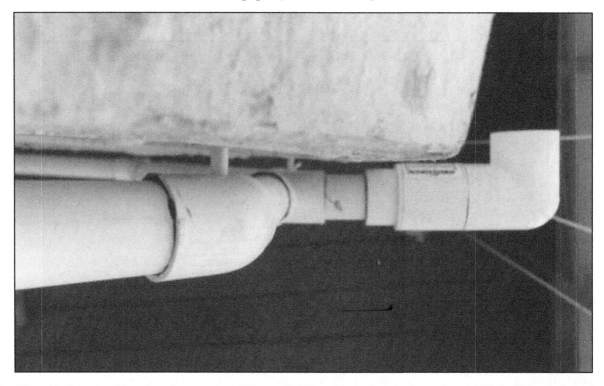

This photo shows the check valves. The bubbler pipe is made of 1 1/2" PVC pipe stepped up to 2" pipe. 2" pipe to the blower improves functionality and prevents potential warranty problems with the blower manufacturer.

Each pipe is cut 22" long. When the 45's on each corner are added, the holes will center at 23". Lay the ring on your forms to locate the holes. The bubbler ring can be attached either before you set your forms in the hole (this makes it a little difficult to attach the 2" line that goes to the blower), or plumb the line completely and prop the forms over the foot well forms (12") allowing you to reach under and attach the spacers and wood screws. Then lower the form down.

IMPORTANT:

Make sure you have an air loop between the tub and the blower. If a check valve is added, be certain to plumb it in the right direction. Check and double check.

The air loop is normally in the equipment area. However, it can be hidden in a wall, or if you're ingenious enough - in the grab rail.

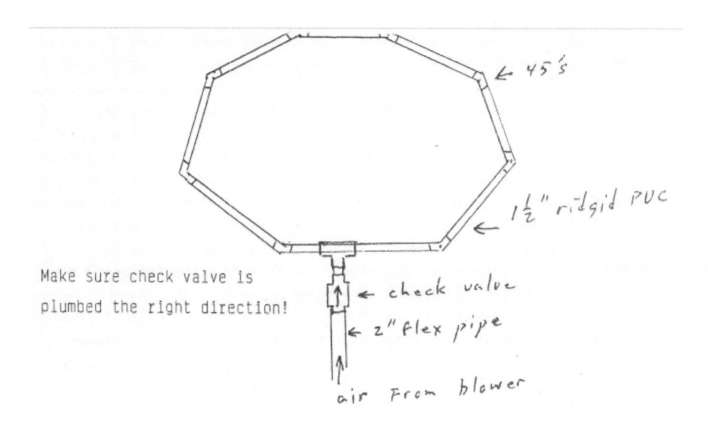

If the blower is located below the tub, then there must be a loop between the tub and the blower. The check valve stops the water when the blower is off. The purpose for this is so that when you turn the blower on, you won't have to push a gallon or two out of your lines. This will also lighten the load on your pump. If the equipment is above and close to the spa, the check valve is not needed; but the loop is.

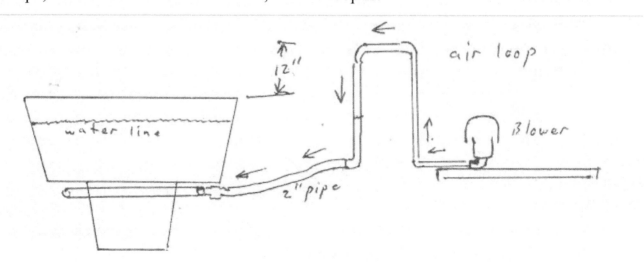

The holes are drilled through the concrete into the bubbler pipe prior to painting. The anchor screws will mark the corners of the bubbler pipe. Know the distance from the back of the seat to the center of the pipe. Allow for thickness of the tile unless you paint. Approximately 40 holes 1/8".

Tiled tubs are drilled after the tile is in place and grouted.

After the tub is cast and tiled, measure from the back of the seat to find the center of the bubbler pipe. Drill 1/8" holes using a 1/8" carbide drill. Space the holes approximately 6" apart. When drilling these holes, get the drill up to speed and maintain the speed so the drill bit won't seize when it goes into and through the top of the PVC pipe. If you snap off a bit, which isn't hard to do, just mud or grout the hole and start a new one at an angle or along side. If you paint your spa, then drill the holes first, using a larger bit to counter sink them slightly. Paint the spa, then come back and clean the bubble holes out. This gives the spa a better appearance, and prevents exposed edges on the paint. You need at least 40 - 1/8" holes to get proper action and not produce too much back pressure against the blower. A 1/8" carbide bit gives you a hole slightly larger than an actual 1/8". To balance the system, you may need to add a hole or two, and maybe plug one or two, especially the first segment the air enters. The blower must run a couple of minutes to purge all the water out before you can tell how well balanced it is. If it is not perfect, don't worry too much; there will always be one side a little stronger than another.

Here's a tip: When drilling these holes, maintain a steady high speed and don't stop the drill bit when it penetrates the PVC pipe or the hot plastic will seize the drill bit and it will snap. Have several bits on hand.

In a tiled tub, the bubbler holes are drilled last. Holes are 1/8" and 6" apart on this tub. If you can, drill through the grout lines. Then if you break a drill bit or make a mistake, you simply grout the hole. If you break the tip of a drill bit and you want the same hole, start again in the same hole, but at an angle to avoid hitting the broken bit.

Note: A 1/8" carbide drill will make a hole slightly larger than an actual 1/8".

13 ~ AIR BUTTONS

These air buttons are located on the pump house wall.

Air buttons are on the deck.

In this installation, the air buttons are on a wall. The board can be removed if a button requires replacement.

Air buttons are on the edge of top of the tub. This tub is 22" above floor.

Air buttons are on the side of a bench.

Air Switches

If at all possible, mount the air switches on a wall or on a deck within easy reach of the spa. The air buttons are rubber and they will need to be replaced occasionally.

Rubber air button

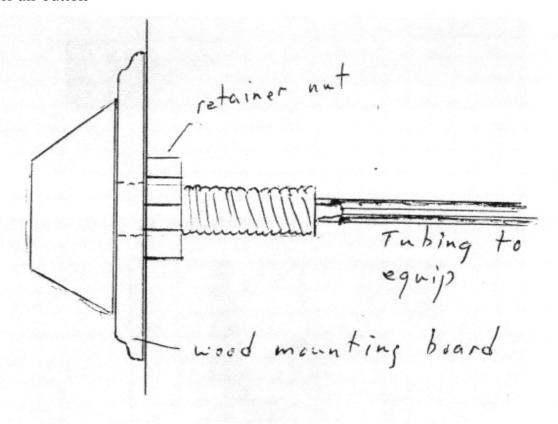

Note: Don't crimp the tubing.

There are some situations where the air buttons must be on the tub. Then, as illustrated, you will need to set them up in such a manner they can be replaced when needed.

The air buttons and the skimmer are next to step.

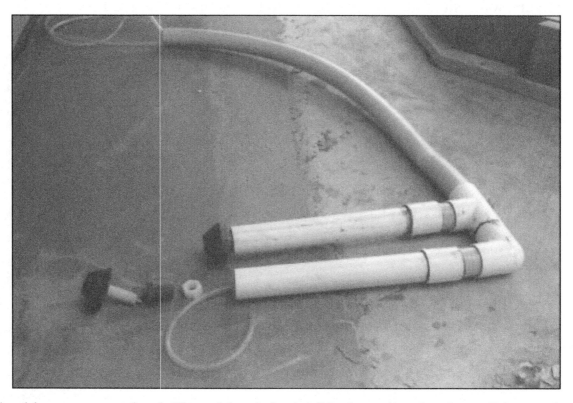

The bushings are not glued. The tubing is in 1 1/2" pipe, allowing it to slide so when the buttons are attached and replaced, you don't crimp it.

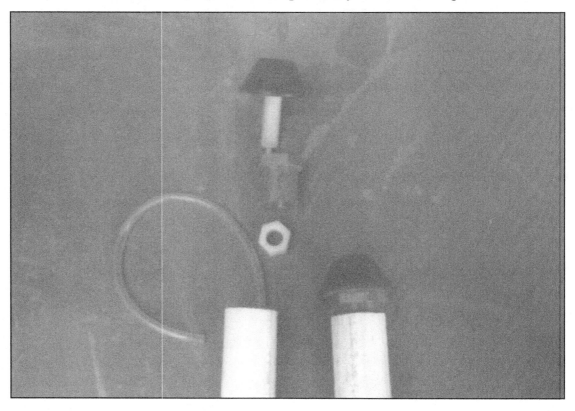

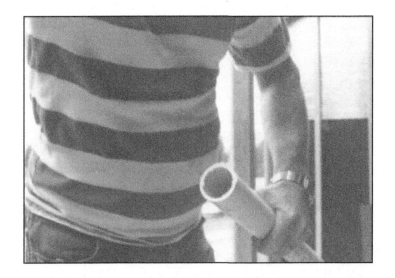

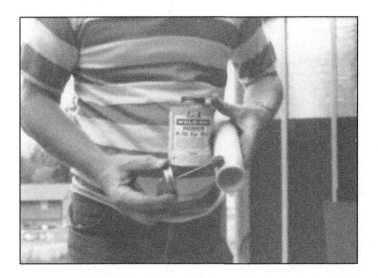

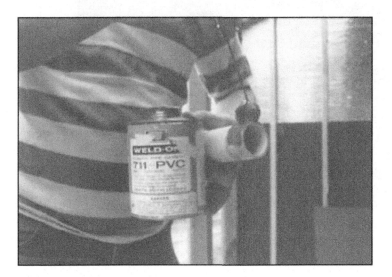

The proper way to glue PVC pipe:

1. Read the instructions on can.

2. Clean burrs from the ends of the pipe.

3. Use a primer, especially on flex pipe.

4. Use a glue formulated for the pipe you are using. Don't skimp. Use liberal amounts on both pieces being glued (fresh glue only).

5. Insert the pipe immediately and hold in place for 30 seconds to a minute.

6. Let it cure before putting to use.

7. Have plenty of ventilation. Don't breath the fumes, and don't smoke or use around an open flame.

8. After gluing a blower, wait 24 hours before turning the motor on. The fumes, when fresh, are explosive.

Note: When gluing a blower, wait 24 hours before turning the motor on. The fumes are explosive when fresh.

14 ~ ELECTRICAL

Before beginning, you must know if your home can handle the load that a spa places on your electrical panel. If it is inadequate, then consider a natural gas or propane gas heater. The heater demands the most energy. A typical 220V, 6KW skid package will draw about 40 amps and a 220V, 11.5KW skid package about 60 amps. A gas skid package will draw about 20 amps (220V). It is better and cheaper to operate 220V equipment than 110V. It can be cheaper to use gas heat rather than upgrade your electrical panel. If your electrical panel can take the extra load then an electrically heated spa will do the job fine. Gas packages cost a little more than all electric.

Note: Skid packages include the pump, heater blower, filter and electric switches. Lights are separate and 110V.

Spa Light and Grounding

Spa lights are usually in the foot well, under or opposite to the steps. Either spot is fine. I use the same niche locating that is used in most plastic spas, and mounting it in the same manner with screws, with one exception; I don't cut a large hole in the forms. Mounting instructions come with the lights. A ground wire is attached to the outside of the niche. If plastic conduit is used, a ground wire attaches to the inside of the light niche. The cord to the spa light also has a ground. There will be 3 grounds to the spa light, and the circuit for the light must be on G.F.I. (ground fault interrupter). The spa light switch must be at least 5' from the spa.

Grounding

The re-bar must be grounded. The grab rail and/or its anchors must be grounded; the light and light niche, and any metal near the spa. In most cases, a #8 bare copper wire is attached to the rebar by circling the tub and attaching it in at least 4 places with clamps, and a loop reaching up to attach to the spa rail and the end to the light niche.

Check the electric codes pertaining to your area. Have a qualified electrician do all of the electrical work. Have it inspected!

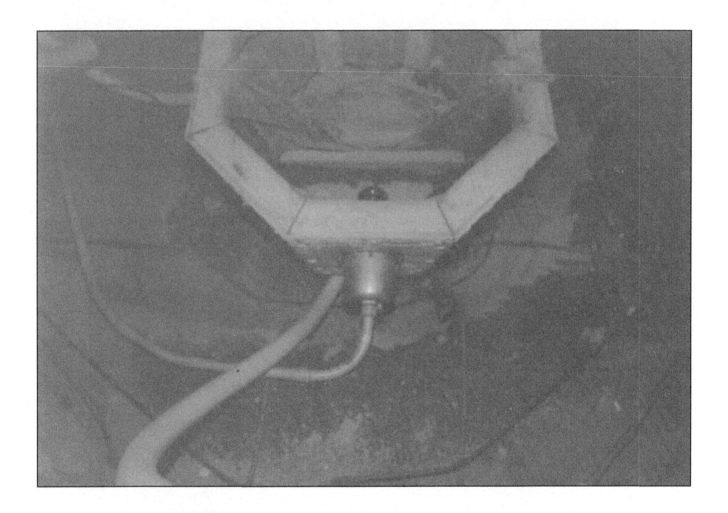

Keep bends in the conduit to the spa light gradual. Plastic pipe can be heated to bend.

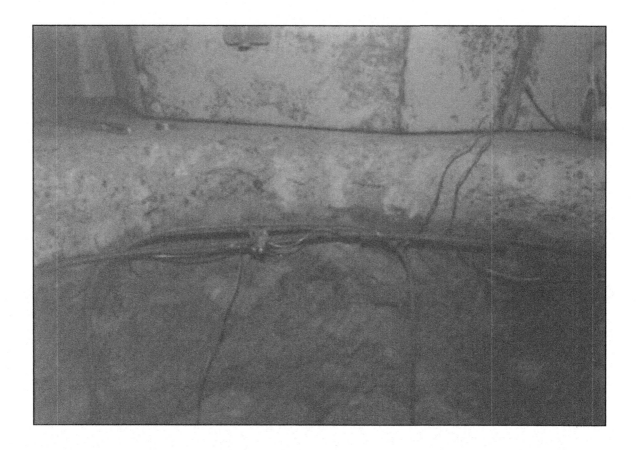

The ground wire is clamped at least 4 places around tub. Notice the loop sticking up; this will attach to the grab rail. Wire is continuous without any splices.

~ ~ ~

NATIONAL ELECRICAL CODE
ARTICLE 680
IV. Spas and Hot Tubs

680.40 General. Electrical installations at spas and hot tubs shall comply with the provisions of Part I and Part IV of this article.

680.41 Emergency Switch for Spas and Hot Tubs. A clearly labeled emergency shutoff or control switch for the purpose of stopping the motor(s) that provide power to the spa.

680.42 Outdoor Installations. A spa or hot tub installed outdoors shall comply with the provisions of Parts I and II of this article, except as permitted in 680.42(A) and (B), that would otherwise apply to pools installed outdoors.

(A) Flexible Connections. Listed packaged spa or hot tub equipment assemblies or self-contained spas or hot tubs utilizing a factory-installed or assembled control panel or panel board shall be permitted to use flexible connections as covered in 680.42(A)(1) and (A)(2).

(1) Flexible Conduit. Liquid tight flexible metal conduit or liquid tight flexible nonmetallic conduit shall be permitted in lengths of not more than 1.8 m (6 ft).

(2) Cord-and-Plug Connections. Cord-and-plug connections with a cord not longer than 4.6 m (15 ft) shall be permitted where protected by a ground-fault circuit interrupter.

(B) Bonding. Bonding by metal-to-metal mounting on a common frame or base shall be permitted. The metal bands or hoops used to secure wooden staves shall not be required to be bonded as required in 680.26.

(C) Interior Wiring to Outdoor Installations. In the interior of a one-family dwelling or in the interior of another building or structure associated with a one-family dwelling, any of the wiring methods recognized in Chapter 3 of this Code that contain a copper equipment grounding conductor that is insulated or enclosed within the outer sheath of the wiring method and not smaller than 12 AWG shall be permitted to be used for the connection to a motor, heating, and control loads that are part of a self-contained spa or hot tub or a packaged spa or hot tub equipment assembly. Wiring to an underwater luminary shall comply with 680.23 or 680.33.

680.43 Indoor Installations. A spa or hot tub installed indoors shall comply with the provisions of Parts I and II of this article except as modified by this section and shall be connected by the wiring methods of Chapter 3.

Exception: Listed spa and hot tub packaged units rated 20 amperes or less shall be permitted to be cord-and-plug- connected to facilitate the removal or disconnection of the unit for maintenance and repair.

(A) Receptacles. At least one 125-volt, 15- or 20-ampere receptacle on a general-purpose branch circuit shall be located not less than 1.83 m (6 ft) from, and not exceeding 3.0 m (10 ft) from, the inside wall of the spa or hot tub.

(1) Location. Receptacles shall be located at least 1.83 m (6ft) measured horizontally from the inside walls of the spa or hot tub.

(2) Protection, General. Receptacles rated 125 volts and 30 amperes or less and located within 3.0 m (10 ft) of the inside walls of a spa or hot tub shall be protected by a ground-fault circuit interrupter.

(3) Protection, Spa or Hot Tub Supply Receptacle. Receptacles that provide power for a spa or hot tub shall be ground-fault circuit-interrupter protected.

(4) Measurements. In determining the dimensions in this section addressing receptacle spacing, the distance to be measured shall be the shortest path the supply cord of an appliance connected to the receptacle would follow without piercing a floor, wall, ceiling, doorway with hinged or sliding door, window opening, or other effective permanent barrier.

(B) Installation of Luminaires, Lighting Outlets, and Ceiling-Suspended (Paddle) Fans.

(1) Elevation. Luminaires, except as covered in 680.43(B)(2), lighting outlets, and ceiling-suspended (paddle) fans located over the spa or hot tub or within 1.5 m (5 ft) from the inside walls of the spa or hot tub shall comply with the clearances specified in (B)(l)(a), (B)(l)(b), and (B)(l)(c) above the maximum water level.

(a) Without GFCI. Where no GFCI protection is provided, the mounting height shall be not less than 3.7 m (12 ft).

(b) With GFCI. Where GFCI protection is provided, the mounting height shall be permitted to be not less than 2.3 m (7 ft 6 in.) over a spa or hot tub:

(1) Recessed luminaires with a glass or plastic lens, non-metallic or electrically isolated metal trim, and suitable for use in damp locations

(2) Surface-mounted luminaires with a glass or plastic globe, a nonmetallic body, or a

metallic body isolated from contact, and suitable for use in damp locations

(2) Underwater Applications. Underwater luminaires shall comply with the provisions of 680.23 or 680.33.

(C) Wall Switches. Switches shall be located at least 1.5 m (5 ft), measured horizontally, from the inside walls of the spa or hot tub.

(D) Bonding. The following parts shall be bonded together:

(1) All metal fittings within or attached to the spa or hot tub structure.

(2) Metal parts of electrical equipment associated with the spa or hot tub water circulating system, including pump motors.

(3) Metal raceway and metal piping that are within 1/2 m (5 ft) of the inside walls of the spa or hot tub and that are not separated from the spa or hot tub by a permanent barrier.

(4) All metal surfaces that are within 1.5 m (5 ft) of the inside walls of the spa or hot tub and that are not separated from the spa or hot tub area by a permanent barrier.

Exception No. 1: Small conductive surfaces not likely to become energized, such as air and water jets and drain fittings, where connected to metallic piping, towel bars, mirror frames, and similar nonelectrical equipment, shall not be required to be bonded.

Exception No. 2: Metal parts of electrical equipment associated with the water circulating system, including pump motors that are part of a listed self-contained spa or hot tub.

(5) Electrical devices and controls that are not associated with the spas or hot tubs and that are located not less than 1.5 m (5 ft) from such units; otherwise, they shall be bonded to the spa or hot tub system.

(E) Methods of Bonding. All metal parts associated with the spa or hot tub shall be bonded by any of the following methods:

(1) The interconnection of threaded metal piping and fittings.

(2) Metal-to-metal mounting on a common frame or base.

(3) The provisions of a solid copper bonding jumper, insulated, covered or bare, not smaller than 8 AWG.

(F) Grounding. The following equipment shall be grounded:

(1) All electrical equipment located within 1.5 m (5 ft) of the inside wall of the spa or hot tub.

(2) All electrical equipment associated with the circulating system of the spa or hot tub

(G) Underwater Audio Equipment. Underwater audio equipment shall comply with the provisions of Part II of this article.

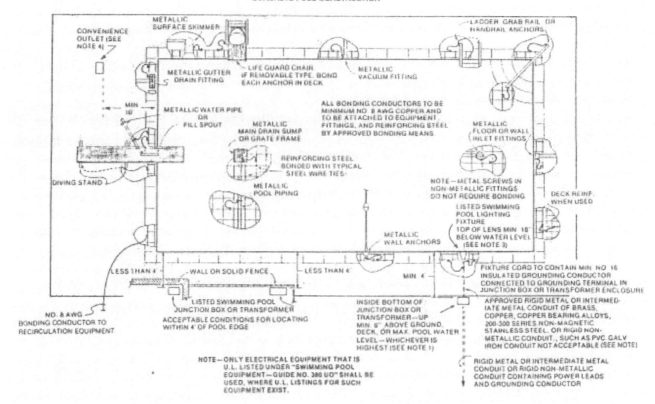

15 ~ OUTER DAMS

The 2 x 4's on the deck are the outer dams. They determine the height and width of the top edge of the spa. Notice the concrete will overlap the edge of the deck approximately 1 and ½ to 2". The width is not only determined by the thickness of the walls, but by the tile you may plan to use. See the notes on tile. If you plan to paint the entire spa, you may want rounded edges. This can be done by adding curved molding to the forms or by mudding later.

The outer dams must be level.

Some are simple (above) - some are not (below)

16 ~ POURING THE CONCRETE

There are several options for pouring concrete. For my first hot tub, I bought several 60-80 lb bags of concrete from Home Depot. To each bag in the mixer, I added one shovel of Portland cement. The water I used was from 5-gallon buckets with 8 ounces of air entrainment mixed in. Visit a store that carries concrete material and buy 5 gallons of air entrainment chemical. The store will explain it. This additive will prevent the concrete from spalling and cracking in the winter. Start with enough bags of concrete to make 3 cubic yards. If it looks like you are running short, send someone to get more. You should have one or two helpers, a wheelbarrow, a cement mixer, and a few 5-gallon buckets. When the concrete mix has filled the area around the footwell and under the seats and starts up the walls, stop for a period until it starts to stiffen. When that happens, go ahead and fill the forms to the top.

If you use a commercial truck, do the same. This will be a very wet pour. Order pea gravel and sand. A pumper's mix is 60% sand and 40% pea gravel. Add air. It is a 5-6" slump. In the order, request a 6-sack mix.

Notice the plastic garbage cans are full of water. This adds ballast; added insurance that the forms won't rise up. Here we are using the good old wheelbarrow.

Below, we build a chute for concrete delivery.

Prior to pouring the concrete, check and recheck everything. Have everything ready before you even think about calling a cement truck out. Use bolts if you don't want to invest in 'C' clamps. Always order concrete in the morning if at all possible. You will need approximately 4 yards of concrete for this size spa, with enough left over to pour a pad for the support system.

Plastic garbage cans with water add ballast - extra insurance that the forms won't rise up.

For the anchor bolts, mix your own concrete (approximately 6 to 12 - 60lb bags of pre-mix or 1/3 yard of concrete). When pouring the spa, order a cement truck with approximately 4 yards of 5 or 7 sac cement pea gravel mix and add air (Darnex), 7" slump or wetter. You want a very wet mix so it will flow in and around your forms and plumbing.

I prefer not to use a stinger. Instead, I use a 3' piece of 1 1/2" flex, glued to a 5' piece of 1 1/2" rigid PVC to agitate the concrete. With a wet mix all you need to do is shake the mixture a little as it's flowing under your forms and you won't have any rock pockets. If you use a stinger, be very careful or you will destroy your forms.

If you pump your concrete, the mixture will be determined by the pump operators, and pumping usually vibrates enough so you won't have to agitate at all, provided it's a wet mix.

As the concrete is flowing under and around your forms, watch that it doesn't load up too much on one side or your forms will be shoved over to one side. You will probably get some movement and the forms will stretch upward a little.

Nail spacers between the spa forms and the outer forms to maintain the same distance. This is also an easy way to control the air vent pipes.

Don't forget to set the grab rail. Maker sure the ground wire is attached. The grab rail can be set solid or install anchors while the cement is fresh for the removable rail. <u>Make sure the ground wire is attached to the anchor.</u>

Your outer dam should be level. Pour the concrete and trowel the outer dam. The spa forms will move a little and you can't rely on them to stay level. Next, trowel the top edges as flat as you can. After the cement stiffens up, you can finish troweling the top edge. The better job you do here, the easier it will be to tile. If you want to slope the edge for water drainage, now is the time. Now keep the top moist; don't allow the concrete to dry too fast. Leave the forms on for at least 3 days. This will allow the concrete to cure without drying too fast. Remember, this is a wet pour. After pulling the forms off, dry the cement slowly and avoid temperature extremes.

Usually, after I pull the forms, I fill the tub with water. Leave the water in for one or two days. This is a perfect way to check the level of your spa; mark the water line so when you tile, it's accurate. The water helps in curing the concrete and will leach out salts and chemicals from the concrete. Drain the water out. Now is the time to add steps inside, elevate seats, and touch up the top edge with topping mix if it is not level all around the top edge of the spa. Let the spa dry approximately 4 days before tiling. If you plan to paint with epoxy, the concrete should be plastered with thin-set mixed with acrylic, then allowed to dry per instructions.

17 ~ PAINTING AND TILING

Painting your Spa

Painting, of course, requires a paint designed for concrete pools.

The surface must be prepared as the instructions on the paint can call for. An epoxy paint will give a very smooth and durable surface.

Tiling

Tile is more expensive than paint, and requires a lot more labor, but it gives you the most durable surface you can put on a spa.

All Tile

Tile and light blue paint

When doing any job, there are always several ways to do it; and tiling is no different. There are certain steps that must be followed.

1. The surface must be prepared; clean and flat (chip high spots down).

2. Use the best materials available.

3. Use a tile that will stand constant water and durable enough to withstand some exposure. Discuss this with your tile distributor.

4. Attach the tile by using a thin set mixed with 100% acrylic. There are several on the market. Get your supplies from one source if possible, so your thin set grout and add mixtures are compatible.

5. When laying tile, eye appeal is very important. Grout lines must be the same and straight. Watch for tiles that are crooked or a wavy surface. The tile will show the flaws in the surface.

6. Let your wife or significant other choose the colors and design.

7. Study rule number 6 again.

8. Use a level and make sure your water line is level or it will show up like a sore thumb. You can cheat a little with your grout lines, but only a little; and it helps if you use dark grout with dark tile and light grout with light tiles.

9. A sanded grout is a little rougher than non-sanded, but will hold up much better.

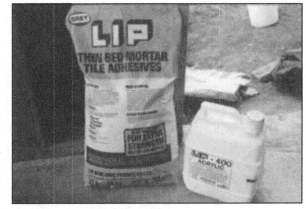

10. Mix your grout with a latex or at least 50% acrylic and water. I prefer, on many jobs, to use 100% acrylic with the grout.

11. You should have your tile on hand before you start the tub to assure availability and to plan the width of the tiled rim. If at all possible, you will want to use whole tiles on top.

12. Balance the segments of the tub to be tiled. In other words, if your tub is an octagon, each section should have the tile centered in the same manner.

13. Make sure the tile you purchase can be cut or you may have to rent a diamond saw.

14. If you are cutting a pattern tile and the cut ruins the pattern, or the patterns won't line up, use a sold color where the corners meet.

15. Plan your tile so you will know how the corners will come together. An easy way, if you haven't tiled before, is to lay out all of the tile first and cut all of the corners before mixing any adhesive.

16. Patterns will help with mosaics and thin bars.

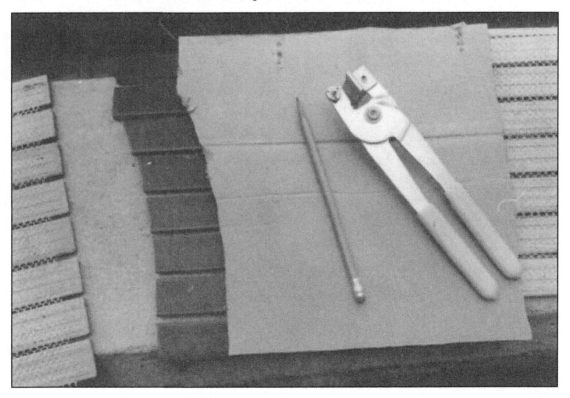

17. Work small areas at a time. Step back every now and then and look at your work.

18. Use masking tape to mark your cut lines if pencil doesn't mark. The tape here keeps the tile from moving.

19. If you are working alone, it may take a full day to do the top rim.

20. It may take another two or three days to finish tiling the inside. Clean the surface as you go.

21. Grouting takes time. Clean the surfaces continuously. Dark grout will stain, so either grout the top before doing the inside, or tape and mark off the inside.

22. After the grout cures, grind all the cut edges and any sharp points with a grinder. Now is also the time to drill the holes for the bubbler.

23. Allow the tile work to cure for a few days prior to filling the tub with water. You must use heaters if the temperature is below 40° F.

24. The steps may be slick and you may want to use a non-skid tape. In a public use spa, you must use a non-skid tile on steps and/or non-skid surface tape.

25. The first time you fill the tub, the water will cloud as materials from the tile and adhesives dissolve. After 2 or 3 days, change the water and it should stay crystal clear with the correct maintenance of the spa chemicals.

18 ~ SUPPORTING EQUIPMENT

The standard size spa will have a skid package that usually consists of a 1 1/2 hp two-speed water pump. a blower, an electric or gas heater, propane or not. The equipment is skid mounted and pre-wired. Also included will be a 50 sq. ft. cartridge filter. There are several on the market. You can also have one delivered to your home at competitive prices.

This book was originally published in 1985. Since then it has become more difficult to find complete "skid packs." A pool or spa company can likely build one for you. The other option is to build your own.

Equipment for a hot tub is your biggest expense. It used to be every spa dealer had skid packs. These have the pump, filter, heater, and blower on a frame, and wired. You could hook these up and everything was there. You probably won't be able to find one pre-assembled because of liabilities, as one wants to manufacture these, but you can buy your own components and assemble your own skid. Have a qualified licensed electrician wire it.

A basic system consists of a 1.5 hp 2-speed spa pump, a cartridge or sand filter, an electric or gas heater, a blower, a spa light, and air switches. See the following illustrations.

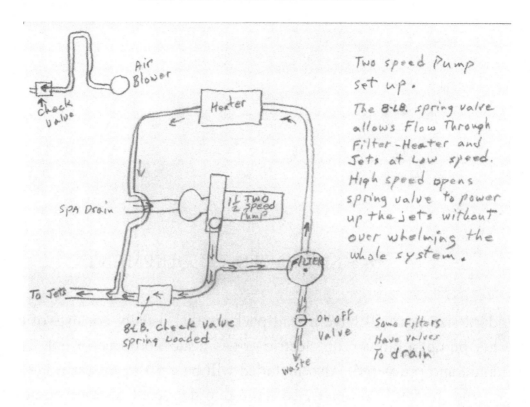

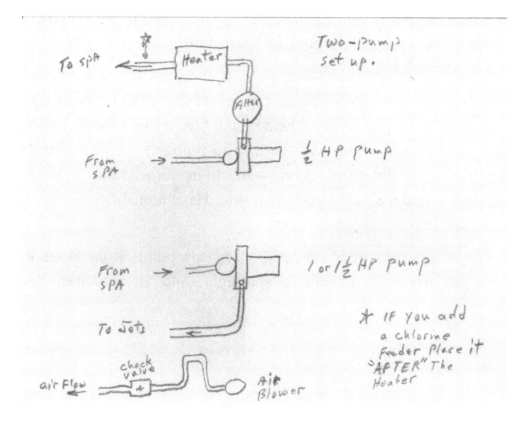

19 ~ EQUIPMENT PAD

The average equipment pad is 3 1/2" deep and 4' wide. If your plumbing is encased in concrete, remember not only the spa plumbing, but also the spa light, air switch tubing, drain, etc. Another method is to block out an area 10" x 16" to accommodate all the plumbing, etc.

The above pad is larger (7' wide) for a gas-heated spa. Notice the groove for a downspout.

Blocked out and tunneled for plumbing.

Nails in the 2 x 4's hold the pump house in place. Nail to the undersides, leaving 1/2 of the nail in the wood; then set the 2 x 4's in the fresh cement.

The pads for a gas-heated spa are larger. They are 7' wide to accommodate placing the heater along side the pump house. If you enclose a gas heater, then you will need a chimney and you'll also have to vent the enclosure. If possible, leave the heater outside. They are designed for it, and you'll be able to insulate your equipment and plumbing for minimum heat loss and quiet operation.

20 ~ PUMP HOUSE

The pump house is essential. It serves several functions:

1. Protection from the weather.

2. Protection from theft or from tinkering.

3. Prevents loss of heat. An insulated pump house will greatly reduce operating cost. The

greatest expense of a spa is in the heating. Even if you equipment is indoors, the equipment should be insulated in some kind of box. You will also derive some benefit of the heat given off by the water pump, which operates over 100° F. Because pump motors do get hot, the pump house should not be absolutely air tight or too small. If it is, then drill holes to provide ventilation for the motors. The blower motor will create a vacuum if you try to seal your pump house too tightly.

4. An insulated pump house will greatly reduce unwanted noise from the equipment.

5. When you turn the blower on the initial air will be warm until you exhaust the air in the pump house then it will cool down to the outside air. Picture it being 10° F outside and you turn the blower on. If you didn't have a pump house you would get 10° air immediately. That would feel like someone dumped ice cubes on you.

6. If your pump house has a pad, do not touch the house, so it won't transmit vibrations from the equipment. The equipment could be on a bedroom wall and you won't hear the pump at the low speed.

7. You can build a pump house with a flat top with Formica for a roof and use it as a table along side your barbeque.

This pump house is 3 1/2' by 4' wide at the base. The back is 4' high and the front is 3' high. The top is plywood covered with starter shakes and a 2 x 4 frame that fits into the pocket formed by framing. The top lifts off to give you access to the filter. The filter cartridge lifts out the top of the canister. The front is held in place by two dead bolts. The entire box is lined by 1 1/2" Styrofoam.

Note: A sand filter will necessitate a larger pump house.

Roof is starter shakes on plywood.

The equipment must be maintained, so allow for easy access.

The pump house should have a light inside.

21 ~ ROOMS, SKIRTS, AND DECKS

This concrete patio is designed for a future room. The pump house is made so it would be flush to a future wall and would not interfere. The corner of the patio is formed to accommodate a 34" window unit and there is room for a floor drain. The window can be removed and replaced by a 6' slider, giving direct access to the house.

1. Build the spa and patio first.

2. The following year, put on a roof.

3. The following year, enclose in a room.

4. The following year, finish off the room's interior, tile the floor, etc.

By planning a spa in this way, you can work with smaller amounts of money, and who knows - you may really like having the spa outside.

Depending on where you live, a roof may be a necessity for the rain.

Inviting isn't it? Spas that are convenient to use, ARE USED.

A spa in a bathroom has some advantages. This is a special set-up for a person in a wheelchair. I feel most people want their bed and bathrooms private, and locate the spas on a deck or near a recreation room.

Decks and Skirts

Not everyone wants their spa level with their deck. The solution is either a two level deck, or skirting. These skirts are very easy to build, and they are made the same way for either a concrete or acrylic spa. Because decks are built in so many ways, the following pictures are ideas that you may be able to use. The construction is the same for a concrete or plastic spa.

This deck is 12' x 12'. The octagon skirt is 8' across. The skirt height is 17 1/2". The tub with the top cover adds about 5" to the total height. Keep this in mind as it may obstruct a view.

The pictures tell the story. First you box the spa area in. Then the corners are cut in.

These floor joists are treated 2 x 6's on 16" centers.

The beams are 4 x 6 fir. Floor joists are 2 x 10. concrete blocks are used around the tub and in the corner.

Most of the deck is nailed in place. The center boards are positioned after the spa is in place. That makes it easier to set the tub and hook up the plumbing.

The center boards are spaced and cut to length, then removed. A collar is made and nailed in place.

Plumbing is attached, then the tub is lowered. If the area is tight, then sand is dumped through the area left open through the deck.

Notice the end beams are different. This was done to match the look of the existing deck.

Note: All measurements are taken from inside surfaces.

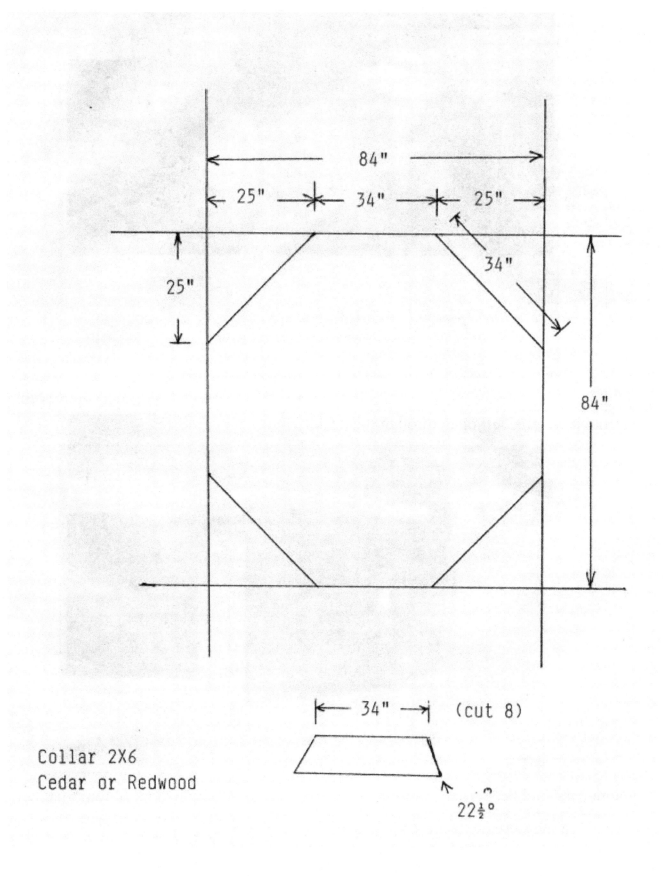

Treat all wood with a preservative.

Bottom nailers and corners first.

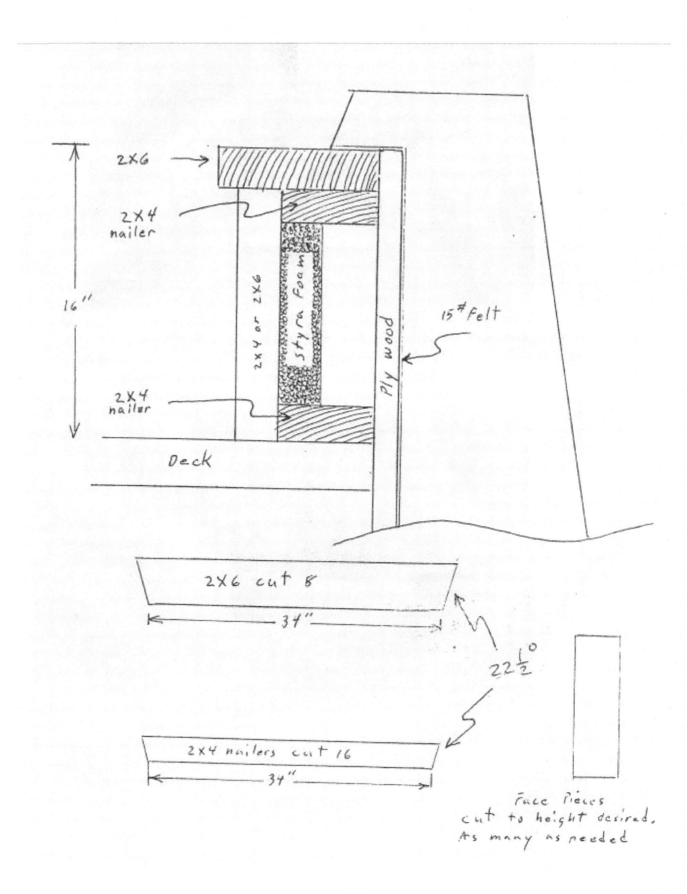

This frame was made up first and moved around so the owner could decide where they wanted their spa.

The height of this set up was decided by the depth of the hot tub, height of deck above the ground.

Add a step and you have a nice set up.

Or without a step you have a nice set up.

22 ~ STAYING HAPPY AND HEALTHY IN YOUR SPA

The following chapter on staying happy and healthy in your spa and hot tub is developed by the Seattle-King County Department of Public Health.

Reprinted by permission.

Introduction

Some cultures, such as the Japanese, have long realized the physical and psychological benefits of soaking in hot water. Now Americans are also discovering the pleasures and benefits of the hot tub and spa.

Soaking in a hot tub can be soothing and relaxing. The warmth relaxes muscles and promotes blood flow to the skin and in the limbs. Many people find that this comfortable experience helps them to rest and manage stress. Some find this to be energizing.

You can appreciate the benefits of your hot tub even more when you know it is being used and maintained correctly. This brochure will provide you with guidelines for the safe use of your hot tub so you can enjoy your tub and avoid most hazards or risks.

For example, bacteria, algae, and fungi love the warm water of your tub. They prosper in moist, warm environments, and can spread infection and disease. The hot water in a hot tub can also be a potential health hazard. Water which is too hot can be harmful, especially if you or your bathers are pregnant, have any circulatory problems, heart disease, are on certain medications, or have been drinking alcohol.

That's why it is very important that you properly use and maintain your hot tub. A well-operated hot tub can bring you many years of enjoyment and satisfaction.

Definition

In this brochure, we call them by their popular name: spas and hot tubs. They can also be called whirlpools, Jacuzzis (a brand name), hydro-therapy, or soaking tubs. These are large tubs or small pools which hold hot water for people to soak in, not bathe. Some are equipped with whirlpool jets and bubblers for underwater massage. They are made of wood, concrete, tile, plastic or fiberglass. There are many sizes, brands and types, but they all require careful use, operation and maintenance.

This information is for use primarily with single family residential spas and hot tubs, and should be followed in conjunction with the manufacturer's instructions that came with the equipment. Everyone in your household helping to maintain the hot tub should read this booklet thoroughly. Public spa operators such as those in health clubs, apartments, and condominiums, should consult their local health department for information regarding the correct operation of their facilities.

Use Your Spa and Hot Tub Safely

Water Temperature: Hotter is Not Better!

The water of your hot tub should not be warmer than 104°F. Always keep an accurate thermometer in the tub water because your hot tub's thermostat may be in error. Use a high-quality shatterproof thermometer with at least one-degree increments.

Water which is too hot can raise the body temperature high enough to cause heat stroke (the body's inability to regulate its internal temperature), this can be fatal even to healthy adults, if you have any questions about your own fitness or ability to soak in a hot tub, check with your physician.

A temperature of 100°F-104°F is considered safe and comfortable for a healthy adult. Most healthy adults can enjoy this water temperature for as long as desired, although it may raise the body temperature to the water temperature, and eventually become more uncomfortable (like a fever). At higher water temperatures, the soaking time should be shortened; for example, limit your soak to a maximum of 15-20 minutes at a water temperature of 104°F. If you are planning a long rest in the tub, lower the temperature closer to normal body temperature, about 99°F. Some people find even lower water temperatures useful as an energizing experience. Try different water temperatures in the 98°F- 104°F range until you find what suits you best.

One way to prevent overheating is to not submerge your entire body in the hot tub water. Keeping your arms and shoulders out of the water is a good way to keep from getting too hot.

The surrounding air temperature will also affect the way your hot tub water feels, especially for outdoor tubs. On hot or cold days, the hot tub water may seem warmer or cooler than it really is. Therefore, always check your thermometer for the true water temperature before adjusting your water heater. The point is that you should not rely on your estimate of the water temperature because you may inadvertently raise the temperature too high for safety.

Checking your thermometer is also protection against the possibility of a faulty heater thermostat.

Special caution on water temperature is recommended for young children; their temperatures rise faster than adults. Children's small bodies cannot absorb much heat, and their sweat glands are not fully developed.

Pregnant women should be careful to limit their hot tub soaks to 10-15 minutes at a maximum water temperature of 102°F. Longer soaks can raise the body temperature high enough to cause fetal damage, particularly during the first three months of pregnancy (possibly resulting in a child with brain damage or deformity). Women in their child-bearing ages may want to note this precaution in the event they may be pregnant and not know it.

Do Not Use Alcoholic Beverages During Tub Use

Despite the popular image of people in hot tubs drinking wine or other alcoholic beverages, do not use alcoholic beverages before or during hot tub use. Alcohol is a depressant which causes slowed reflexes and drowsiness, especially in conjunction with the relaxed soaking in hot water. This can lead to sleep or unconsciousness, and has resulted in drowning.

Hot tubbing with other people is not a preventative measure if they are also drinking and likely to become similarly affected by the combination of alcohol and soaking in hot water. Deaths have occurred from this kind of situation. The spa and hot tub industry has also taken a strong position against mixing hot tubbing and alcohol.

Health Conditions and Medications

Soaking in hot water causes changes in the circulatory system, such as enlargement of blood vessels near the skin. Therefore, people with a medical history of heart disease, circulatory problems, diabetes, or blood pressure problems should check with their physicians before using hot tubs. Additionally, people taking medications causing drowsiness, such as tranquilizers, narcotics, antihistamines, or anticoagulants should not use hot tubs without asking their physicians, due to the risk of drowning described in the previous section. Any drugs and substances which may affect your judgment, or cause drowsiness or sluggishness, should also be avoided while hot tubbing for the same reason.

Preventing an Infection from Tub Water

People with skin, ear, vaginal or other body infections, open sores or wounds should not use a hot tub because of the possibility of spreading infection. Hot water which is not adequately disinfected or maintained correctly can help grow some bacteria and other microorganisms which cause infection. Hot moist skin is also more easily infected. Submerging your head may increase risk of ear, eye or throat infection if the water is not properly disinfected.

One common bacterium called Pseudomonas is usually to blame for the occasional skin infections resulting from poorly maintained tub water. These bacteria are often found in water, so there is no way to prevent them from getting into your tub. Once the bacteria are there, though, you want to disinfect the water to keep the Pseudomonas from infecting the skin. When the chlorine level drops too low the bacteria grow, and can infect the hair follicles, an infection called "folliculitis."

Folliculitis can look serious (although it usually isn't), and it itches, it has been mistaken for chicken pox, flea bites, or scabies. Usually, however, simple folliculitis will heal by itself in 1-2 weeks. The bacteria may sometimes cause additional infections (for example, of deep sweat glands), which then take several weeks to heal. Hot tub bathers who develop an infection should contact their doctors if the problem does not clear up in 7-10 days.

If you get an infection from the hot tub, you will have to drain, clean and disinfect the tub.

Questions have been raised as to whether the herpes virus can be spread through the water in a hot tub (this virus is responsible for a number of conditions, including genital herpes and cold sores). There is currently no medical evidence which suggests that the herpes virus can be transmitted in hot tub water. This virus is spread by direct contact only (e.g. sexual contact for genital herpes).

Similarly, the AIDS virus is not spread through the water in a hot tub. This virus is transmitted only when semen, blood, or vaginal fluids get directly into the blood or mucous membranes of another person through a break in their skin; e.g., during sex, or when needles are shared. The AIDS virus is fragile and is easily destroyed by disinfectants (such as chlorine) used in maintaining the hot tub water.

Shower Before and After Tub Use

All bathers should shower with soap and hot water thoroughly before and after using a hot tub.

Showering before hot tub use is important not only because it washes away many of the common skin bacteria, but also because it removes perspiration, lotions, deodorants, creams, etc. Perspiration and lotions will reduce the effectiveness of the disinfectant (chlorine), and lessen the ability of the hot tub filter to work efficiently because the oils coat and clog the filter mesh. Soaps and lotions can also form foam and scum in the water (this includes suntan lotions, bath oils and soaps, and shampoo). These oils also promote the growth of bacteria. Therefore, rinse well when showering before getting into the hot tub.

Showering after hot tub use will help wash away any bacteria, algae, etc. picked up in the tub which might cause an infection (remember that proper ongoing disinfection will minimize the chance of infection).

Safety and Accident Prevention

Do not allow children to use a hot tub without supervision. Adults should also use caution. As a minimum safety precaution, one person using a tub should have someone within calling distance check the bather regularly. Ideally, a hot tub should never be used alone.

Prevent unauthorized tub use and accidental drowning by keeping a cover securely locked over the tub. Alternatively, install self-closing locked doors to the hot tub area. Outdoor spas should be secured by fences at least five feet high with self-closing gates. Latches should be high enough to be out of the reach of children. Install at least 54" high.

Slips and falls on wet tub and deck surfaces can also cause injury. Do not allow running or roughhousing around your tub. Non-slip surfaces, good deck drainage, steps, and hand holds are important safety features.

Whenever you have beverages around your hot tub, do not use glass or other breakable containers. Broken glass is very hard to remove from a hot tub and usually requires draining all the water.

Injuries or deaths can occur when long hair or a body part is trapped by suction from a drain or outlet whose cover is broken or removed. Children are particularly vulnerable, and they should be closely supervised due to this danger. Broken or missing drain covers should be replaced immediately. If your hot tub has raised drain covers which can snare long hair, make sure long hair is pinned up or at least not flowing loosely. If a child's body is sucked against a flat drain whose grate is broken or missing, the child can be freed by shutting off the pump immediately or placing your flattened hand between the child and the drain to break the suction.

All hot tub electrical equipment should be wired according to the National Electric Code and all relevant local codes under city, county, or state permit. Such work should be inspected by the local jurisdiction for your protection (safety and liability). Additionally, the National Electric Code (and most local codes) require a 120 volt electrical outlet installed between 1 and 15 feet from the hot tub. The outlet must be GFCI (ground fault circuit interrupter) protected to prevent electric shock.

Do not use electrical appliances while using your hot tub (e.g., hair dryers, radios, etc.) in order to avoid electric shock. Battery-operated radios or appliances are good safety measures.

For portable spas and all hot tub electrical equipment, look for a U.L. (Underwriters' Laboratory) listing, which should be clearly displayed on the manufacturer's nameplate.

We recommend having a list of emergency numbers taped to your phone, including your local emergency medical personnel or fire department, and poison control. Include your own address on the list so a non-family member can direct emergency personnel to your home if necessary.

It is also a good idea for you and family members to be trained in CPR (cardiopulmonary resuscitation). Training is available from many community agencies.

Keep up with new developments!

Check with your Spa company or the Product Safety Commission to see if there are any new precautions or recalls. Recently, several drain covers were recalled by manufacturers because the risk of injury and accident was too high.

For the most current information on protective barriers for your spa or hot tub, call your local building department.

Maintaining Your Spa and Hot Tub

Chlorine is the Best Disinfectant

The purpose of using a disinfectant is:

To sanitize the water (kill bacteria and other germs) and to break down (or "oxidize") organic material in the water, such as body oils and perspiration.

Chlorine is the most commonly used disinfectant, and we feel it is the best. It is an excellent disinfectant to preventing the growth of bacteria and algae in the water, and it helps to keep the water clear. Chlorine is available in many forms (it is a gas in its natural state), but is usually available in liquid, granular (coarse powder), and solid forms.

There are various chlorine products available, and you can obtain advice from your pool and spa store on the right kind for you hot tub. Cyanuric acid helps stabilize chlorine against sunlight, so products with a cyanuric acid base are particularly useful in outdoor hot tubs. Your pool and spa retailer can recommend a product without cyanuric acid if you have an indoor hot tub.

Carefully read the labels on your chemical products to determine their content, instructions for storage and proper method for handling, and use. Never mix chemicals, not even different types of chlorine. Many chemicals are not compatible with one another, and may cause an explosion or fire if mixed together. For example, if you have a tablet chorine feeder, never put granular chlorine in it.

We do not recommend using household bleach (liquid sodium hypochlorite) because it may raise the level of total dissolved solids in the water, and it loses strength in storage.

Free Chlorine Residual

Private hot tubs should be maintained at a chlorine level of at least 3 ppm free chlorine residual (ppm means parts per million.)

It is quite tricky to keep the right minimum level of chlorine in your hot tub. Sunlight, heat, bubbling water, perspiration, bodies and body oils cause the release and use of the chlorine from the water. That's why the term free chlorine residual is important. The free chlorine residual is the amount of chlorine which is still in the water after some has been released, used up, or combined chemically with substances in the water. Free chlorine residual is therefore the amount of chlorine which is chemically available to do the job of killing bacteria and algae. You need to check the free chlorine residual level regularly, especially just prior to use, and when the hot tub is being used, to make sure you're keeping the free chlorine residual at 3 ppm or above. Do not use a hot tub with a free chlorine residual below 1.0 ppm, or you will risk catching or spreading infection.

If you had experience maintaining swimming pools, you may notice that hot tub maintenance is different from swimming pool maintenance. The higher water temperatures, aeration jets, and body oils cause chlorine use and loss more quickly than a swimming pool water (as much as four times as fast.) It has been estimated that four adults in a 90°F hot tub can use up to about 3 to 3.5 ppm chlorine in 15 minutes. It is important to note that therefore a tub being used over an extended period of time, such as a whole afternoon or evening will need chlorine added at least every half hour in order to maintain the safe minimum level of 3 ppm free chlorine residual. This will especially be true if there are a number of people using the tub.

After using your hot tub, let the pump filter continue running for one or two hours, and chlorinate the water back up to 3-6 ppm free chlorine residual. (Following a period of heavy or extended use, it may also be helpful to super chlorinate up to 10 ppm to remove chloramines. See next section.) This will destroy bacteria which bathers left in the water, as well as filter out much of the suspended material which people may have on their skin and carry on them into the water.

Although we recommend at least 3 ppm free chlorine residual for hot tubs, some owners maintain their hot tubs at higher levels, e.g., 4-6 ppm free chlorine residual, to provide a greater margin of disinfectant safety. Pool operators have noticed that some gradual bleaching of swimming suits occurs at about 8-10 ppm free chlorine residual, although this poses no health hazard.

Super-Chlorinating

In addition to maintaining your tub's free chlorine residual level at 3 ppm, another important maintenance step is a weekly super chlorination (or "shock treatment") of 10 ppm free chlorine residual.

A weekly super chlorination is useful for removing chloramines, which are substances chemically combined with chlorine ("combined chlorine"). Chloramines are undesirable because they prevent the chlorine from disinfecting properly, and they also cause burning of the eyes and foul odors.

These symptoms are often taken as signs of too much chlorine, but they are actually signs of not enough free chlorine residual. Smell is caused by chloramines, not by free chlorine residual.

The weekly 10 ppm super chlorination will help remove the chloramines. After the super chlorination, allow the chlorine level to drop down to between 3-6 ppm before using the hot tub. (Note: check with your pool and spa store to determine the correct amount of chlorine to add to reach 10 ppm; this will depend on the size of your hot tub. For example, 1 ounce by weight of granular chlorine, such as Dichlor, in 500 gallons of water is equivalent to 10 ppm free chlorine residual in the absence of any chlorine demand.) Use a chlorine product without a stabilizer (such as cyanuric acid) for shock treatment. Your pool and spa retailer may also have other products for this purpose.

Other Disinfectants

There are a variety of chemicals and devices which are advertised as hot tub water disinfectants. Although we strongly recommend the use of chlorine for disinfecting water, some private hot tub and spa owners have used alternative methods. Whichever method you choose, it is very important that you carefully follow the manufacturer's instructions and check with your pool/spa retailer if you have any questions.

Methods of disinfection other than chlorine include: bromine, iodine, ozone, ionization, and ultraviolet light, if you choose to use one of these alternative methods, be sure to ask your pool/spa retailer how to measure and maintain an adequate residual of an effective disinfectant in the water.

Bromine is more popular in spas than in pools. It's related to chlorine and works in a similar way. Bromine combines with organic substances in the spa to form bromamines. Bromamines don't smell like chloramines do, and they do have disinfecting action, which chloramines don't. Too much bromine can result in skin rashes, so be sure to measure the bromine level in your spa.

Ozone is becoming popular for home spas. Ozone is an excellent oxidizer and will kill bacteria and viruses on contact. There is no residual action with ozone. It "cleans" the water that goes through the ozonator, but then the "clean" water goes back in with the "dirty." You'll need to use a disinfectant such as chlorine or bromine in addition to the ozone so that there is a residual in the water at all times. Although ozone should reduce the amount of other disinfectant that you use, it can't be substituted entirely. You'll still need to run tests of your chlorine or bromine, just as you would if you weren't using ozone.

Chemical Balance

Maintaining a proper chemical balance will reward you with clear, clean, fresh-smelling hot tub water. Chemically balanced water depends primarily upon the pH of the water (explained below), the chemicals which help maintain the pH (acid and alkaline chemicals), and water hardness (primarily minerals such as calcium). Soft water may have to be made "harder." Your pool and spa store can advise you about this.

The acidity of water is expressed as a pH value. The pH range extends from 0 to 14; 0 is the most acid and 14 is the most alkaline (or "basic"). Seven is neutral, neither acid or alkaline. The optimum pH of a hot tub is 7.4, with an acceptable range of 7.2-7.6.

Maintaining proper pH balance is important for several reasons. If the pH is too low, it causes skin and eye irritation, staining of the tub's inside surface, and corrosion of metal in the equipment. Too high a pH also causes skin and eye irritation as well as cloudy water. Chlorine is also much more effective in the proper pH range of 7.2-7.6.

Depending on the acidity or alkalinity of the water used to fill the tub and your disinfectant, you may need to adjust your water's pH level by adding an acid or alkaline chemical. For example, adding soda ash or sodium bicarbonate will raise pH. Adding hydrochloric acid or muriatic acid will lower pH. Your pool and spa store can sell you these chemicals and can advise you how to use these products properly.

In addition to the acidity/alkalinity of the water, other measures you may need to adjust are calcium hardness, total alkalinity, and total dissolved solids. Your test kit should measure total alkalinity and will show your tub's level compared to the recommended range show in the chart that follows.

Total dissolved solids, as the name implies, is the level of dissolved substances in the water. This should remain below the recommended maximum of 1500 ppm as long as you maintain proper chlorination, pH, and filtration time, except possibly during heavy use, when you may need to dilute or replace the water if dissolved solids build up too high. Testing of total dissolved solids can be done through a pool maintenance service or private laboratory.

Add fresh water to your tub if splashing or evaporation reduces the amount of water in the tub. Large amounts of water loss by evaporation may cause the remaining water to cloud up since the chemicals and other substances in the water are becoming more concentrated. If this cloudiness does not clear up with the addition of fresh water, chlorine and pH adjustment, and filtration, you may need to drain and refill your tub.

Check with your pool/spa retailer before using scents, salts, or soaps in your hot tub. Scents can hide telltale odors of combined chlorine. This smell should be detectable so you can tell if you need to super chlorinate your tub. Some scents and salts have dyes, which can color your cartridge filter and prevent you from seeing if it's dirty and therefore in need of cleaning. Also, some scents and salts can interfere with the chlorine or may soften the water and upset the water's chemical balance.

Filters, Pumps and Covers

The purpose of your filter is to remove unwanted substances which are suspended in the water, such as algae, dirt, body oils, etc. The filter does not remove all suspended material, but it does remove most of it, and it works with the disinfectant (chlorine) to keep the water clean and clear.

The two major types of filters found with most private hot tubs are: dacron polyester cartridge filters and diatomaceous earth filters. Most private hot tubs come equipped with cartridge filters because they are easier to use and maintain by the non-professional.

The cartridge is disposable but if kept thoroughly clean it can be reused over several months before being replaced, according to the manufacturer's or seller's instructions.

Operate the filter (with the pump) for at least 3-4 hours a day for the first 7-10 days you run your hot tub, or until the water remains clear for more than 48 hours. After that point, the amount of filtration time will depend upon the size of your tub, pump, and filter, the amount of use, and the manufacturer's instructions. If the water does not remain clear, try increasing the length of filtration time. However, some pumps have two or more speeds so that the pump can be left on at the lower speed to provide constant filtration.

Constant filter operation is important for diatomaceous earth filters because when the water flow is shut off, the diatomaceous earth will fall off the filter leaves (complete instructions on using diatomaceous earth filters should be obtained from your pool and spa store).

You should make sure the water in your hot tub is completely recirculated frequently: e.g., at least every 30 minutes while the tub is being used. (If you do not leave your pump on all the time for constant filtration, turn it on before using to allow the water to recirculate once or twice.) If you are a prospective buyer, make sure the pump you buy is appropriately sized for this purpose, as well as for the number of aeration jets. This way contamination is being constantly removed (although it may not sound pleasant, you should realize that "contaminants" are being introduced into the water every time someone gets into your hot tub).

Do not operate the pump or heater unless the hot tub is filled up to the recommended operating level, if the tub has a skimmer, the minimum water level should be 1" over the bottom of the skimmer opening.

If your hot tub is exposed to freezing temperatures:

The pump should remain operating in low speed during the time that the tub, piping, or support equipment is below freezing temperatures; during prolonged periods of freezing temperatures when the tub is not being used, we recommend that tub, piping, and equipment (pump, filter, heater, etc.) be thoroughly drained according to the manufacturer's instructions to prevent damage.

A floating cover is a good investment for your hot tub because it reduces water evaporation and helps maintain the water temperature (which saves you energy costs). A well-fitting cover also prevents dust and debris from getting into the water, helping to keep the water clear and clean. Floating covers are often an insulating foam product, and if you have an outdoor hot tub, it can be used together with a hard cover to further reduce water and heat loss. A locking hard cover is also a good safety feature, since it prevents children and pets from falling in. You can purchase inexpensive but effective spa cover locks if your cover is not already so equipped. For safety, always remove the cover completely before using your hot tub.

The Test Kit and Chemicals

A test kit is absolutely essential to you for maintaining your hot tub. The test kit allows you to test the water for chlorine levels, pH. and other measures such as total alkalinity.

Test your tub water often enough to help you maintain proper chemical balance. Factors influencing chemical balance include "bather load" (how many bathers use the tub) and, for outside tubs, weather conditions.

The best kit to have is the "DPD" kind, because it can measure the free chlorine residual in your hot tub water. We recommend a test kit with at least four functions, which can measure free chlorine residual, combined chlorine, pH, and total alkalinity. These 4-function DPD kits are made by several manufacturers, and your spa and pool store can help you select one.

Many kits sold to the public are the "orthotolidine' ("OTO") kind and do not give accurate readings at the temperature of the hot tub, and the chemicals (reagents) deteriorate relatively quickly. Most "OTO" kits are 2-function kits, which measure only chlorine and pH. They do not measure free chlorine residual, which is the measurement you need. (Total chlorine is the sum of free chlorine residual plus combined chlorine. Measurement of total chlorine is not the amount available for disinfecting.)

Supplemental test kits are available which measure water hardness. Ask your pool/spa retailer if one is recommended for your area. In soft water areas, keep water hardness high enough to prevent copper pipe corrosion.

The instructions with the test kit should describe how to evaluate the water properly. Test the water before adding tub chemicals to avoid false readings. When mixing tub water and test kit reagents in the kit vial, use the plastic cap (not your finger) to cover the opening. Skin oils from your finger may influence the test results. Read your results immediately after mixing the water sample with test solutions.

Your DPD test kit will probably be set up to measure from 0.2 to 3.0 ppm free chlorine residual. In order to measure chlorine levels above 3.0 ppm, the chlorine scale on the test kit chamber can be multiplied by diluting the test sample of tub water with tap water. For example, fill the test kit chamber half full with sample water, half with tap water; this multiplies the test kit scale by 2. (Therefore, multiply by 2 the reading you see on the test kit to get the actual result.) Since the top level most kits can measure is 3 ppm, anything 3 ppm or above will look the same on the color chart, if you get a measurement of 3 ppm, always run a dilution, since the number could be much higher. If the levels are too high, usually somewhere around 10, you will get no color at all because the chlorine will bleach out the color, if you know you have put in chlorine, and/or you see a flash of pink, run some dilutions. You may actually have a high level that the kit can't measure.

If you use a disinfectant other than chlorine, make sure you ask your pool/spa retailer how to accurately measure your tub's water chemistry.

Adding Chlorine and Chemicals to Your Tub

Self-controlled chemical feeders are available that use a sensor to automatically add the appropriate chemical when needed. This can effectively maintain the appropriate levels of chlorine and other chemicals in your tub water although this can be expensive equipment. Most people intentionally "hand feed" chemicals, using a test kit to measure what the water needs. As long as you are attentive, this will work perfectly well. Somewhat less desirable is a "robot feeder" that adds chemicals at a fixed rate, such as a feed pump or erosion tablets or sticks. Robot feeders do not sense what chemicals the water needs, and depending upon water temperature and how heavily the tub is being used, the standard rate may not be adequate.

When hand feeding more than one kind of chemical to your hot tub, do not mix the concentrated chemicals together. Add chemicals to the hot tub separately and allow several minutes between additions and use the pump, jets and filter to help dissolve chemicals. After adding chemicals, allow at least 30 minutes for all chemicals to dissolve and disperse before using the tub.

Hot tub chemicals in liquid form may be added directly to the tub water; measured amounts can be poured in slowly just above the water level to avoid splashing. Dry chemicals should be dissolved and diluted first. (Pre-dissolving chemicals is particularly important for wood and gel-coated fiberglass hot tubs.) Dip a clean plastic bucket of water out of the hot tub, and add the proper amount of dry chemical to the water in the bucket, mixing well until completely dissolved. Then lower the bucket back into the hot tub, pouring the diluted chemical without splashing. Always add chemicals to water, not water to chemicals.

If you use your hot tub over a long period, such as when numerous guests go in and out of the tub over an evening, check the chlorine and other chemical levels at least hourly, then add chlorine or chemicals as needed. High "bather load" can use up chlorine rapidly. Keep bathers out of the tub while adding chemicals and until chemicals are fully dissolved, as described above.

Since hot tub chemicals can burn or poison, store them in their original containers and out of reach of children. Chemicals should be stored in a clean, cool, dry location, away from the hot tub heater. Never store or mix chemicals together; do not even mix different kinds of chlorine together (mixing tablets and granular chlorine products together can cause an explosion); store oxidizers away from organics. Do not smoke around the chemicals, and avoid direct skin contact, e.g., use rubber gloves. Use only clean utensils to handle chemicals; use a separate clean utensil for each chemical.

Cleaning

Your hot tub should be drained about every two months (or according to the size, manufacturer's instructions, and how often the tub is used), cleaned, and refilled with fresh water, due to the buildup of minerals and other substances in the water. Measure and readjust the chlorine level and chemical balance before using the hot tub again.

Some spa and tub manufacturers recommend adding an emulsifier to your tub's water prior to draining it. This breaks up and dissolves oils for easier removal.

To clean your tub, drain it and scrub it out with a 50 ppm (approximately) chlorine solution (1/4 teaspoon Dichlor in 5 gallons of water will yield approximately 50 ppm; mix in a clean plastic pail). Use rubber gloves and long-handled brushes, and be careful to protect your skin and eyes. Avoid inhaling any chemical fumes.

Your cartridge filter should be cleaned monthly, or more often if needed. Depending on the piping arrangement for your tub's filter system, there are one or more indications that the filter needs cleaning:

1. Jet action in the tub will be reduced;

2. Water in the tub will remain cloudy after proper disinfection, and dirt or skin oils may remain on the surface of the water after using the tub;

3. If your filter tank has a pressure gauge, the pressure reading will be 5 psi or higher than the reading when a clean filter is started when the jets are used.

Disassemble the filter and scrub out the filter housing with the 50 ppm chlorine solution. If you have a cartridge filter, you can clean it in the following manner unless it is due for replacing anyway:

1. Thoroughly rinse down the cartridge with a high-pressure nozzle on a garden hose. Do not clean the cartridge with a brush, because brushing can imbed the dirt more deeply, or even harm the filter fabric.

2. Soak the cartridge for several hours in an oil-cutting solution, such as trisodium

phosphate, or whatever your pool and spa store recommends. Thoroughly rinse the cartridge after soaking. (Trisodium phosphate can burn; follow the label instructions.)

3. Test the cartridge for mineral buildup. Apply a few drops of muriatic acid to the cartridge fabric; if it foams, assume the acid is dissolving minerals (these minerals can plug the filter). To remove the mineral buildup, soak the cartridge in a solution of 1 part muriatic acid to 10 parts water for 2-4 hours. Several cleanings may be necessary for heavy mineral buildup. Rinse well after soaking.

4. Finally, soak the cartridge for several hours in a 50 ppm chlorine solution to thoroughly disinfect it. After soaking, rinse well.

For proper disposal of these cleaning solutions please consult your local sewer district or agency. (In King County, call the Local Hazardous Waste Line) For example, if local regulations allow you to dispose of these solutions in the sewer, dilute them with plenty of water as they are being poured down the drain.

NOTE: If you are on a septic tank system, do not dispose of these solutions in your septic tank. Call your local health department for advice on proper disposal.

CAUTION: These concentrated solutions can burn, so use rubber gloves and goggles and make sure there is good ventilation so you do not breathe the fumes. Rinse off well if splashed on the skin; if splashed in the eye, thoroughly rinse with large quantities of water for at least 15 minutes, and contact your local emergency medical personnel. Keep flushing your eyes with water until assistance arrives.

An alternative method to clean your cartridge is as follows:

1. Rinse the cartridge as described in Step 1 above to rinse loose material from the cartridge.

2. Run the filter through two cycles of your dishwasher. Do not use the heat-dry cycle. Use your regular amount of dishwasher detergent. Turn the filter over for the second wash. The combination of hot water and the caustic dishwasher detergent both sanitizes and removes body oils from the filter pleats. (Do not wash other items in the dishwasher at the same time as the filter.)

NOTE: Check your manufacturer's instructions to make sure this cleaning method is all right for your brand of filter. You may also check with your pool and spa retailer to see if they recommend this cleaning method.

After cleaning the cartridge, reassemble the filter and, if drained, refill the hot tub with fresh water, and apply a "shock treatment" of 10 ppm free chlorine residual for 10 hours.

(Check the chlorine label or ask at your pool and spa store to determine how much chlorine to add to reach 50 ppm and 10 ppm.) Then before reusing the hot tub, carefully measure and adjust the chlorine and pH levels, as needed; make sure the chlorine level is between 3-6 ppm free chlorine residual before reusing.

Some hot tub owners find it helpful to have two filter cartridges; while one is being cleaned by a series of soaks, the other clean one can be in the system so you can enjoy using your tub.

We also recommend that you regularly clean your tub's skimmer (if you have one) of hair and debris after each use. This is important, because the skimmer bucket is an ideal breeding ground for bacteria.

In addition to this regular cleaning, if any bathers report skin rashes from using your hot tub, an additional thorough draining and cleaning of the tub will also be necessary. Follow the same cleaning guidelines just described. Discontinue the use of the hot tub as soon as any bathers report a skin rash or infection. (If you use bromine as a water disinfectant, check the bromine level in your hot tub. Bromine levels which are too high can cause rashes.)

The bathers should contact their doctor's office if the infection does not clear up within 7-10 days. We also recommend reporting the infection to your local health department; you can talk to a Health and Environmental Investigator about the proper operation and cleaning of your tub. Also, for a fee, some health department laboratories or private laboratories will test hot tub water samples you provide for possible sources of the infection. (This testing should be done before cleaning and rechlorinating the tub.) Call the lab for instructions because the water should be collected in sterile bottles, or bottles the lab can provide, and water samples should be delivered to the lab as soon as possible after collection. Refrigerate the water samples since bacteria will continue to grow even at room temperature.

This entire process sounds involved, but some harmful bacteria are extremely hardy and this careful cleaning and disinfecting is necessary to remove harmful microorganisms. You should review your previous operation and maintenance procedures to identify the cause of the infection to prevent further infections and to save yourself the trouble of totally disinfecting the system more frequently than your normal maintenance schedule.

Wood Hot Tubs

If you own a wood hot tub, you may notice that when you first fill your hot tub your water may look reddish brown for a few weeks, in this case, the water is leaching (drawing out) chemicals from the wood. The water should clear up with filtration, extra chlorination and pH adjustment to the appropriate 7.2-7.6 range. Water clarifying additives (sometimes called "polishers") are also available to help clear the water.

We recommend that you clear up this discoloration before using your tub.

Discolored water indicates that there is a "chlorine demand," so there would be a low free chlorine residual for effective sanitation. A new wood hot tub will use much more chlorine initially for this reason than it will later on.

Foam may develop on the water the first few times you use your tub. Foam is an indication of oils or resins in the water. Chlorine will normally remove these substances, if necessary, add an emulsifier to help remove them. De-foaming products are available; these are oil-based substances. This oil, like body oils and lotions, can reduce the hot tub's filter efficiency, may require more frequent cleaning of the filter, and can promote bacterial growth.

In time, some wood hot tubs may develop a white, fibrous matting on the inside walls where the wood is in contact with the water. This matting is bleached and frayed wood fibers due to the chlorine in the water. This may indicate excessive chlorine and improper pH, although a properly maintained hot tub may also develop this matting. Ordinarily, this matting is not a health hazard as long as the surface of the wood remains smooth, and the pH and chlorine levels are maintained on the correct level. A clean, smooth surface will prevent splinters, and will prevent the formation of crevices or pockets to protect bacteria and algae from chlorine.

Other Kinds of Hot Tubs or Spas

You will want to follow additional maintenance procedures for your hot tub which the manufacturer or seller recommends. This will depend on the material your hot tub is constructed of. The previous section, for example, describes several points for owners of wood hot tubs.

Acrylic and fiberglass hot tubs should be maintained according to the manufacturer's instructions, or scratching or blistering may result. For example, do not use abrasive cleaners to clean the surfaces of acrylic or fiberglass hot tubs, because this may damage the tub material. Gel coated fiberglass tubs will require regular waxing, especially if scratched, and you should use the special waxes sold for this purpose (do not use household wax.) Gel coat is a porous surface, and waxing provides an impervious coating. Waxing can also be a regular maintenance step for acrylic tubs, and it helps to keep a nice luster. The gel coat on fiberglass hot tubs also may need servicing if it becomes blistered; contact your pool and spa store or a fiberglass repair business for assistance if repairs are necessary.

The purpose of being careful with the maintenance of your tub's surface is to maintain a clean, fairly smooth surface so there are no scratches or pockets to protect bacteria and algae from chlorine.

Portable spas contain smaller quantities of water, which means that increased attention to mater maintenance is important. For example, buildups of combined chlorine tend to occur more rapidly in portable spas, and more frequent "shock treatments" will therefore be necessary.

If You are on a Septic System

If you are on a septic tank system and are planning to put in a hot tub or spa, contact your local health department to see if any special regulations apply, if you have already installed your tub, this section describes some special procedures you should be aware of.

Do not drain most or all of your hot tub water into your septic system at one time. Large amounts of water suddenly emptied into a septic tank can "overwhelm" the system. This can cause sludge from the tank to wash into the drain field, clogging the pipes, and water may back up into your home. (This does not apply to homes on a public sewer system, if your home is on a public sewer system, your hot tub should be hooked up to a drain into the sewer, not the yard.) If your local plumbing or health code requires your tub to be connected to your septic tank system, drain your tub water over a 3-5 day period, after allowing the chlorine level to drop to 0.5 ppm or below.

If local codes permit, when you empty your hot tub for cleaning, or for other reasons, slowly and carefully drain the water onto land (e.g., onto a lawn or into shrubbery) as follows:

Chlorinate your hot tub to 1.0 ppm free chlorine residual and then let the water sit without use until the free chlorine residual level drops to 0.5 ppm or below, before draining the water onto the ground. As long as this water has been chlorinated, it is not harmful and can safely be emptied into your yard. Avoid draining the water around grass or shrubbery if the free chlorine residual is as high as 3.0 ppm. A high chlorine level can harm some plants. Also, it is easier on plants if the water is not hot, but allowed to cool to room (or outside) temperature. (Also be careful not to drain the water close to fish-bearing waterways, including storm drains and ditches which empty into streams, because chlorinated water will harm fish.)

If you do drain your tub's water in your yard be careful not to do so in your septic tank's drain field area. The ground may become too wet to properly absorb the drainage from the pipes in the drain field. (If you would like more information about the proper maintenance of septic tank systems, contact the Environmental Health Office in your local health department.

Water from backwashing a diatomaceous earth filter should be backwashed through a separation tank, which will prevent the diatomaceous earth from getting into the septic tank system and plugging it up. The earth can be thrown away in the garbage, and the water drained onto the ground. Backwash water of 3-5 gallons will not harm your septic tank system, but use care not to empty all of the hot tub water into the septic tank. (Most private hot tubs come equipped with a cartridge filter which does not require backwashing, so this procedure may not apply to you.)

Installing Your Hot Tub

If you have not yet installed your hot tub or spa, here are a few points to remember:

1. We recommend having all utility work (plumbing, gas electric) done by licensed workers under appropriate permits issued by your local government. This is the best way to assure safety and to prevent potential problems with incorrect piping or wiring. Additionally, many insurance policies will not cover mishaps unless the work has been done by a licensed worker under an appropriate permit. Consider the building codes and inspections have been developed for people's safety; therefore, use your permit as an opportunity to make sure your tub and equipment is being installed safely and correctly.

2. Arrange to drain your tub according to local regulations. We generally recommend that unless your plumbing is on a septic tank system, plumb your tub to drain into the sewer, not the storm drains or into the yard. An acceptable alternative is to siphon or pump drain water into a sink which drains into the sewer. Drain water from the tub should be considered waste water, and should be treated in the sewage system. Never drain tub water in or near fish-bearing waterways.

3. Remember to look for a U.L. (Underwriters' Laboratory) listing on equipment you purchase, if you are purchasing a portable spa, the entire spa should bear the U.L. listing.

4. There should be a vacuum breaker installed in your equipment used to fill and drain your tub. This vacuum breaker (or "air gap") will prevent any back siphoning of tub water into your drinking water system. For more information, contact your pool or spa retailer or your local health department.

Quick Summary of Recommended Levels

	Recommended Level	Acceptable Range	Other Comments
Chlorine (Free Chlorine Residual)	3 ppm minimum	3 ppm minimum	weekly super chlorination
pH	7.4 (approx.)	7.2 - 7.6	
Water Temperature	100°F for healthy adults, 15-20 minutes	104°F max. for healthy adults	Low temps and shorter soaks for children, pregnant women
Total Alkalinity wood tubs plaster & tile tubs/spas vinyl, painted & fiberglass tubs/spas	80-125 ppm 80-125 ppm 125-150 ppm		
Calcium Hardness wood tubs plaster & tile tubs/spas vinyl, painted & fiberglass tubs/spas	150-200 ppm 150-200 ppm 150-200 ppm		
Total Dissolved Solids	1500 ppm maximum		

Ideal Conditions and Troubleshooting

	Ideal	Problem	Action to fix problem
Odor)	Light, fresh clean odor	Foul smell or heavy chlorine odor; eye burning	Test for free chlorine residual level; adjust as necessary after a 10 ppm super chlorination to remove chloramines.
Water Clarity	Clear, clean water; light blue-green color	Cloudy or colored water; foaming	Increase filtration time; if you have tried that, clean your filter and filter equipment. Also, check pH and chlorine levels and adjust. If necessary, replace tub water.
Water "Feel"	Smooth, silky feel	Slimy or "hard" feel	Check pH, chlorine, and total alkalinity levels and adjust if necessary. Increase filtration time.

Acknowledgements

This brochure was originally developed by Benjamin Leifer, M.P.H., Public Health Educator, and the following Environmental Health staff: Sharon Greenman, R.S., Larry Kirchner, R.S., Carolyn Boatman, R.S., and Robert Howell, R.S. The assistance of the following individuals is gratefully appreciated: James C. Brown, M.S., R.S.: Nancy Phillips, R.S., Gary Fraser, R.S. The generous assistance of the following hot tub and spa industry representatives is deeply appreciated: Alice Cunningham and Blair Osborne of Olympic Hot Tub Co., Jane Marx of Spa Hut, Robert Wisenberg of Water World, and Sharon Hayes of King Distributors. Subsequent editions have been updated by the Public Health - Seattle & King County with assistance from many hot tub/spa industry representatives. The assistance of Jerry Bjork of the Seattle Office of the Consumer Product Safety Commission is also appreciated.

23 ~ USING LEFTOVER CONCRETE

Make mushrooms.

Yard decorations or yard lights.

Or a table and chairs.

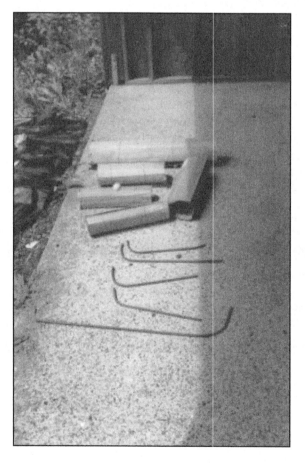

Materials:

A. Concrete, stiff enough so it won't pour.

B. Plastic visquine 3 to 5 mil.

C. Cardboard.

D. Short pieces of re-bar.

Scoop out a depression about 2 feet in diameter.

Cover the depression with plastic.

Fill the depression with concrete, then place cardboard tubes. Insert re-bar and with a garden trowel fill the tube. Remember the stem should be long enough to bury one half in the ground.

Large table size mushroom must have a very long stem. If they toppled over they could easily injure. Small mushrooms have 6" diameter stem and a table size should have a stem 8 to 10" diameter. Fold cardboard in an irregular manner. The more irregular the more natural they look. The depression should be irregular and for realism at lines for gills.

Before the concrete sets, roll over the edges so you don't end up with knife sharp edges.

Place in the garden around your spa. As they age, their appearance will improve.

ABOUT THE AUTHOR

After a successful career as an air traffic controller, Marv Johnson founded Wishing Well Tile and Spas in 1985. In addition to hot tubs and swim spas, he has built public fountains and a lavish mountain resort spa. He is a talented designer, artist, and craftsman whose masterpieces have been featured in Sunset Magazine and Pool and Spa News. In his spare time, Marv can be found playing a round at his favorite Pacific Northwest golf course.

www.wishingwellspas.com
marv@wishingwellspas.com

Made in the USA
Las Vegas, NV
03 January 2022